Literary Pilgrims

The accident that started the Taos artist colony:
Ernest Blumenschein with broken wagon wheel.
Photo by Bert Phillips, September 4, 1898.
Courtesy Palace of the Governors (MNM/DCA).
Negative no. 40377

LITERARY
PILGRIMS

**The Santa Fe and
Taos Writers' Colonies
1917–1950**

Lynn Cline

UNIVERSITY OF **NEW MEXICO** PRESS   ALBUQUERQUE

©2007 by the University of New Mexico Press
All rights reserved. Published 2007
Printed in the United States of America

12   11   10   09   08   07   1   2   3   4   5   6

Library of Congress Cataloging-in-Publication Data

Cline, Lynn.
  Literary pilgrims : the Santa Fe and Taos writers' colonies, 1917–1950 /
Lynn Cline.
     p. cm.
  Includes bibliographical references and index.
  ISBN-13: 978-0-8263-3851-8 (pbk. : alk. paper)
  1. Authors, American—Homes and haunts—New Mexico—Santa Fe.
  2. Authors, American—Homes and haunts—New Mexico—Taos.
  3. Authors, American—20th century—Biography.
  4. New Mexico—Intellectual life—20th century.
  5. New Mexico—In literature.
  6. Literary landmarks—New Mexico.
  I. Title.
  PS144.N35C65 2007
  810.9'9789—dc22
  [B]
                        2006029418

Design and composition: Melissa Tandysh

Opening chapter illustrations are details from the Walking/Driving
Tour Maps of Santa Fe and Taos, created by Shirley Lynn.

For my husband, Kyle,

with love and gratitude,

and my dad, Tony Cline,

for always serving up

huge helpings of inspiration . . .

From the beginning, from that first night when we stood out in the dry cold under the brilliant winter sky, and I felt the tremor of recognition, Santa Fe was to be for me the place of Poetry.

—May Sarton, *A World of Light*

Contents

Preface ix

Introduction 1

Chapter One: Fertile Ground 8

PART ONE: IN SANTA FE

Chapter Two: Alice Corbin Henderson 21

Chapter Three: Witter Bynner 29

Chapter Four: Mary Austin 42

Chapter Five: Willa Cather 52

Chapter Six: Oliver La Farge 61

PART TWO: IN TAOS

Chapter Seven: Mabel Dodge Luhan 73

Chapter Eight: D. H. Lawrence in Taos 87

Chapter Nine: Mabel Dodge Luhan,
    After D. H. Lawrence 96

Chapter Ten: Spud Johnson 103

Chapter Eleven: Frank Waters 117

PART THREE: A MEMORABLE LITERARY LANDSCAPE

Chapter Twelve: Significant Others   127

    Lynn Riggs   127
    Raymond Otis   130
    Haniel Long   132
    Erna and Harvey Fergusson   135
    Paul Horgan   140
    Fray Angélico Chávez   142

Conclusion: The End of an Era   145

Walking/Driving Tours   152

    Santa Fe   152
    Taos   158

Notes   165

Bibliography   174

Index   178

Preface

THE IDEA FOR a book about the writers who lived and worked in Santa Fe and Taos from the early 1900s to the beginning of World War II struck me not long after I moved to Santa Fe in 1993. I discovered that not only had literary luminaries such as D. H. Lawrence and Willa Cather spent time here, they had interacted with a fascinating group of writers in Santa Fe and Taos I had never heard of who wrote passionately about the region. Through poetry, prose, memoir, and story, these writers memorably captured a region and its rich and varied blend of cultures. Their work reached audiences around the country, often convincing readers to travel to New Mexico so that they themselves could experience the unforgettable landscape and cultures.

Because they wrote about similar themes, joined forces to promote their work, and founded groups to keep the traditions and art forms of regional cultures intact, these writers in Santa Fe and Taos created authentic literary colonies, which shared traits with art colonies that arose in Woodstock, New York; Carmel, California; and elsewhere in America during the same era. Like their counterparts in these other colonies, the writers in northern New Mexico hoped to establish a haven from an industrialized, commercialized American culture they believed to be corrupt and soulless. Santa Fe and Taos seemed ideal locales where writers could achieve this goal.

While some of the books these authors wrote remain in print, much of their work has been lost or neglected. To a great extent, the history of these literary colonies has been eclipsed by the art colonies of Santa Fe and Taos that flourished at roughly the same time and helped lay the groundwork for the thriving art scene of contemporary Santa Fe. The city's art market has become so famous that the legacy of the art colonies outshines that of the literary colonies. More people today, for instance, probably recognize the names of artists Georgia O'Keeffe, Ansel Adams, and John Sloan than the names of writers Alice Corbin Henderson, Mary Austin, Mabel Dodge Luhan, and Witter Bynner. In fact, a professor I studied with in New Mexico once insisted that Santa Fe poet Witter Bynner was a woman. (He wasn't, and the mistake only underscored the extent to which Bynner's fame had faded, along with the reputations of many of the other Santa Fe and Taos writers who were his contemporaries.)

The Santa Fe and Taos writers of this era led intriguing lives and produced compelling work that focused on the Southwest. Some of their homes and the places in which they gathered for social and literary events still stand, often only slightly altered, illuminating the layered history of the literary colonies. Much of their work remains in print and those books now out of print often are found in libraries, used bookstores, and the collections of bibliophiles. These volumes bear seeking out because they reveal a golden era of northern New Mexico literature. The lives and legacies of these writers deserve to be better known. After all, their work brought recognition to the region and helped pave the way for the lively literary scenes that currently exist in Santa Fe and Taos.

This is not to say that other books have not been written about these New Mexico writers. Indeed, this book could not exist without the notable books that have come before it, especially Lois Palken Rudnick's fascinating biographies of Mabel Dodge Luhan and her famous Taos estate, and Marta Weigle and Kyle Fiore's history of the Santa Fe and Taos writers' era.

In addition, the following people generously donated their time, knowledge, and assistance to the research phase of this book and I thank them with all my heart: Art Bachrach, Sam Ballen, Saul Cohen, Letitia Frank, Dr. Estevan Rael-Gálvez, Earl Ganz, Peter Goodwin, Pen La Farge, Jack Loeffler, Meredith Machen, John Macker, John

Nichols, Nathaniel Owings, Mary Powell, Lois Palken Rudnick, Sue Sturtevant, Sharyn Udall, Sallie Wagner, Barbara Waters, Marta Weigle, Chris Wilson, and David Witt. Nita Murphy, the helpful librarian of the Southwest Research Center of Northern New Mexico in Taos, offered a wealth of information and a wonderful place to work, as did the owners and staff of the Laughing Horse Inn, Hacienda del Sol, the Mabel Dodge Luhan Conference and Retreat Center, and the Inn of the Turquoise Bear. I also am grateful for the help provided by Tomas Jaehn of the Fray Angélico Chávez History Library; Mary Jebsen of the Museum of Fine Arts; and the employees of the State Library of New Mexico and the Santa Fe Public Library, which maintain well-stocked Southwest reading rooms. Santa Fe artist Shirley Lynn provided the wonderful maps for the Santa Fe and Taos tours, and for assistance with obtaining the photographs, I am indebted to Mike Kelly and Kari Schleher of the Center for Southwest Research at the University of New Mexico; Steven Schwartz of The Witter Bynner Foundation for Poetry; Jim Smith and Carl Condit of Sunstone Press; Gerald Peters, John Macker, and Catherine Whitney of the Gerald Peters Gallery; Sherry Carlton of the Harwood Museum; Joe Traugott of the Museum of Fine Arts; Cary McStay and Daniel Kosharek of the Palace of the Governors Photo Archives; and Shelby Miller of Santa Fe. I also greatly appreciate the literary treasures and inspiring conversation found in Nicholas Potter's bookshop, Dorothy Massey's Collected Works Bookstore, Leo Romero's Leo's Art Books, and Helen Macleod of Books & More Books. The book could not have been written without the support of The Witter Bynner Foundation for Poetry, which graciously provided a grant. David Brownlow, Nancy Brown, and the rest of the gang at Studio X offered a productive place to work. A heartfelt thanks to Luther Wilson of the University of New Mexico Press for believing in this book and to Jill Root, my excellent copyeditor. And last, but never least, I thank my trusted readers—Peggy van Hulsteyn, Robert Nott, and Rachel O'Keefe Bohlin—for their encouragement and sage advice; my brother Hugh Cline and my stepmother Hilary Hays, for unwavering support and love; my father Tony Cline for invaluable insight, handy humor, the gift of wisdom, and the ability to always be there; my mother, Pat Cline, who died in 1991 and somewhere, I hope, is smiling over this book; and my darling husband, Kyle, whose love, humor, and patience with this project I appreciate more than words can ever express.

Introduction

SANTA FE HAS long been a major tourist mecca shaped by the allure of the exotic. Its intriguing myth of ancient culture, rugged beauty, and alternative lifestyle has, across the centuries, captured the imagination of the explorer, the adventurer, the seeker, the outcast, and the artist. The same is true of Taos, though on a smaller scale. Starting at the close of the nineteenth century, however, the appeal of these two towns grew particularly potent, drawing countless sojourners and settlers who possessed highly creative artistic aspirations.

Artists and writers of every ilk started trekking to northern New Mexico in the early twentieth century, fleeing a modern world obsessed with war. Weary of a culture marred by excessive materialism, greed, corruption, and mechanization, these Southwest newcomers found hope for a better future in the ancient traditions of the Pueblo, Navajo, and Hopi people they encountered, as well as with the Hispano people who had put down roots in New Mexico generations earlier. They firmly believed that living in this remote part of the country offered an antidote to America's focus on urbanization, industrialization, and preoccupation with military power starting in the World War I era.

Accessing the remote high desert of the Sangre de Cristo Mountains a century ago required infinitely more time, courage, and physical strength than it does today. Voyagers made the arduous journey by

The Inn at the End of the Trail
In Old Santa Fe

Open the Year 'Round

The Harvey Company   *David L. Cole, Manager*

Illustration of La Fonda from advertisement in *Laughing Horse*, no. 20,
Summer 1938. Courtesy Gerald Peters Gallery Bookstore.

carriage, horse, or primitive railroad cars, which first serviced Santa
Fe in 1880. The train stopped in Lamy—eighteen miles southeast of
Santa Fe, seemingly in the middle of nowhere—and passengers pro-
ceeded to town on a branch line that rode directly into Santa Fe. (After
the branch line closed in 1926, a Harvey House car shuttled passengers between Lamy and Santa Fe, where guests could stay at La Fonda,
one of Fred Harvey's famous railroad-era hotels.) First-time visitors
generally shared the sentiments of poet Alice Corbin Henderson, who
arrived via the train from Chicago in 1917 for tuberculosis treatment
and immediately proclaimed Santa Fe "simply glorious."[1]

Indeed, northern New Mexico's dry desert air, forested mountains,
and flat-top mesas have wielded a rough sort of magic on its denizens,
from the ancient ancestors of the Pueblo people to sixteenth-century
Spanish explorers, nineteenth-century traders of the Santa Fe Trail, and
the lively group of prolific writers who established literary colonies
in Santa Fe and Taos from the early 1900s to the outbreak of World
War II. These writers arrived on the heels of a group of national and

international artists who had founded their colonies in Santa Fe and Taos a few years earlier. In both towns, the writers and artists frequently collaborated on projects as well as personal achievements, creating books, magazine articles, and group exhibitions along with marriages, families, and friendship. They often joined forces to fight for or against social and political causes as well. Their steady output of literature and art defined their years in the Southwest as a virtual golden era.

As Pulitzer Prize–winning author Paul Horgan once wrote, experiencing the Southwest could be devoutly spiritual—especially in Santa Fe, situated at 7,000 feet and surrounded by the foothills of the Rocky Mountains: "Vision receives it all with a sense of new power. The earth seems near to the heavens, and in the light of sun, moon or stars, even its distant features can be discerned strangely well—by night, in all their flowing contours, by day, in all their color."[2]

The writers who trekked to northern New Mexico from America's big cities as well as from Europe during the first quarter of the twentieth century experienced a similar sense of awe upon viewing Santa Fe and Taos. In their search to escape America's crass commercialism and Europe's bleak, war-torn wasteland, they embraced an isolated region, rich with rare and unfamiliar cultural traits. These celebrated intellectuals—including British author D. H. Lawrence, American author Willa Cather, American poet and naturalist Mary Austin, and American poet Witter Bynner (famous in his heyday but nearly forgotten now)—saw no place for themselves or their work in urban centers and industrialized societies. They rejected, for example, employment en masse in factory jobs, which they viewed as monotonous, unimportant, and numbing to mind, spirit, and heart. In their search for new possibilities and fresh subject matter, these writers shunned major cities, regarding them as "a turbulent reminder of the power of the nation-state to steamroll its populace into 'mindless conformity' and to reduce human life to rubble in its capacity to make war," according to American Studies scholar and author Lois Palken Rudnick.[3]

New Mexico appealed to writers, as well as artists, for numerous reasons. Many of them suffered from tuberculosis, and the high, dry climate offered a place to recover from illness as well as the vagaries of twentieth-century America. They also found inspiration in an unfamiliar terrain inhabited by indigenous people whose cultures remained inextricably tied to the land. And they sought solace in a remote and relatively unpopulated place of strange beauty. Not every first-time visitor fell under Santa Fe's spell, but those who did decided to stay, often for the rest of their lives.

The magnetic pull of northern New Mexico's landscape and culture on the writers and artists of the colony era was not uncommon. In the early part of the twentieth century, a similar sort of power also propelled creative people into forming acclaimed art colonies in other appealing parts of the country, most notably Provincetown, Massachusetts; Carmel-by-the-Sea, California; and Woodstock, New York. In an essay about the Woodstock Art Colony, which by 1923 had become a famous art center known as the "Woodstock Whirl," scholar Karal Ann Marling noted that most of America's art enclaves sprang up between 1880 and 1910, primarily because one or two landscape artists happened to stumble upon an area of natural beauty, or a group of creative people united expressly to establish a counterculture far from the dehumanizing aspects of America's teeming cities.[4]

In northern New Mexico, two painters venturing westward stumbled upon Taos in 1898 after their wagon wheel broke and thus were born the art colonies of Santa Fe and Taos. The literary colonies followed suit when Alice Corbin Henderson arrived in Santa Fe in 1916, followed by Mabel Dodge Luhan in Taos in 1917. The essential elements identified by Marling as key to the formation of America's art enclaves also existed in the Southwest: enough writers settled in Santa Fe and Taos to form small colonies in both places, and the populations frequently expanded when other writers visited and, becoming smitten, stayed longer than planned.

Not everybody found inspiration, though. Some of the writers who first sojourned to New Mexico seeking health or inspiration for their work left after a brief visit, disgruntled by life in a small town where damaging gossip, petty rivalries, personal dramas, and a busy social calendar interfered with creativity. Others recognized the career pitfalls inherent in living so far from New York and the East Coast, the acknowledged heart of America's literary life. Those who did stay, however, found it impossible to return to their old lives in Chicago, Los Angeles, New York, or elsewhere.

Undeniably, life in the Southwest forever changed the colony writers. They, in turn, left a lasting influence upon the region as well as outside of it. Their poetry, prose, and art trumpeted a fascinating portrait of northern New Mexico to the outside world. Largely because of work that emerged from the Santa Fe and Taos literary and art colonies, the region was billed as an attractive alternative to a civilization bankrupted by greed, commercialism, industrialization, war, and a loss of faith.

Ironically, though, extolling the region had major repercussions. The artists and writers attracted by the land and its unique cultures had settled in a place barely touched by modern America. Yet through their work they furthered the evolution of Santa Fe and Taos into authentic tourist towns, with all of the common trappings. Their artful depictions of the ancient cultures and timeless traditions drew countless tourists carrying the baggage of the very civilization these artists and writers rejected. The predictable pattern of discovering an unsung place worth knowing, only to witness curious trend-followers overrun the locale into near ruin, played itself out in Santa Fe and Taos too. Nonetheless, the myth was established: Northern New Mexico was a fabled land that could unfetter minds and set hearts free.

The myth persists today, drawing writers who stay either for a spell or a lifetime. New Mexico has worked like a balm on those with a desire to write, from retired journalists who have become best-selling mystery authors to contemporary poets who, like Santa Fe colony poet Alice Corbin Henderson, discovered their voices upon moving to the Southwest.

A look at the lives of the most significant writers of the Santa Fe and Taos colonies reveals a fascinating portrait of a thriving literary era. The writers working in these small towns produced poetry, essays, novels, plays, and nonfiction works about northern New Mexico that appealed to readers nationwide as well as around the world. Their output attracted writers from all parts of the country and, in the case of D. H. Lawrence, from across the Atlantic. Although they frequently collaborated on projects, these writers often fought bitterly, divided by jealousies, disappointments, rivalries, and other typical problems in small communities where large and sensitive egos interact on a daily basis.

Literary Pilgrims begins with a brief discussion of northern New Mexico history that focuses on literature but by no means explores every facet of the state's fascinating past. Subsequent chapters introduce the major writers who produced work during the fertile decades of the Santa Fe and Taos writers' colonies as well as a handful of authors peripherally connected to the colonies. Part 1 of the book explores Santa

Pueblo Indian Dancers (drawing)   *by D. H. Lawrence*

"Pueblo Indian Dancers," D. H. Lawrence drawing from *Laughing Horse*,
no. 13 (1926). Courtesy Gerald Peters Gallery Bookstore.

Fe writers, while Part 2 devotes itself to those in Taos. The chapter
arrangement mirrors as closely as possible the chronological order in
which the writers settled in New Mexico.

The Santa Fe and Taos writers interacted on a regular basis, contributing to a sense of community even as they feuded among themselves.
Despite their tendency to socialize, organize as political and cultural
activists, and fall into feuding, the literary colonists still found ample
time to create a body of regional work that remains unparalleled in
northern New Mexico's literary history.

The book concludes with walking and driving tours of Santa Fe and

Taos that visit former homes, gathering places, and other sites open to the public connected to the literary colony figures.

Literary Pilgrims celebrates the wonderful world of literature inspired by New Mexico. Countless writers have recorded their indelible impressions of this land and undoubtedly many more will find new words and novel ways to continue the legacy.

CHAPTER ONE

Fertile Ground

Pueblo Indian Roots

NEW MEXICO'S RICH literary history stretches across the ages, firmly rooted in ancient indigenous cultures thriving in the Southwest centuries before the first official printed book, the Gutenberg Bible, rolled off the press in 1456 in Mainz, Germany. Ancestors of the Pueblo people settled in northern New Mexico some 10,000 or more years ago, along and near the waters of the mighty Rio Grande. They lived in rhythm with the seasons, never doubting that the natural world held potent power. The stories they have told for generations not only pass along cultural traditions; they reflect the role of nature in their culture. Pueblo tales, for instance, depict ravens, coyotes, and other creatures as deities and portray rivers, rocks, wind, and other elements of nature as spiritual aspects of the planet's life force.

When Swiss-born anthropologist Adolph Bandelier began to study Pueblo culture, he felt compelled to write down what he learned. He recorded his findings in his 1880 novel *The Delight-Makers*, which reconstructs prehistoric Native American culture in the Southwest, focusing on the Koshares, a powerful secret society known as the Delight-Makers. His book remains a classic, one of the first to explore America's indigenous people.

Like the ancient Greek and Roman myths or Old Europe's early folk and fairy tales, Native American stories remain vibrant today, reflecting age-old beliefs to a modern world. More recently, Native Americans have started recording their stories and beliefs in books for native and non-native readers alike. N. Scott Momaday, of Kiowa heritage, paved the way when he won the Pulitzer Prize in 1969 for his poignant novel *House Made of Dawn*, about a young Native American soldier returning home to a New Mexico reservation after World War II. Since then, contemporary Native American authors including Leslie Marmon Silko, Louise Erdrich, Linda Hogan, Joy Harjo, Jim Welch, and Sherman Alexie have achieved success with contemporary native and non-native literary audiences alike.

Spanish Colonial Foundations

The Hispano population of northern New Mexico shares an equally rich literary tradition. Indeed, one of the very first published poems to emerge from the region was written by Don Gaspar Pérez de Villagrá, a member of Don Juan de Oñate's late-sixteenth-century expedition from Spain into New Mexico. The epic poem, "Historia de la Nueva Mexico," penned in thirty-four rhymed cantos, celebrated Oñate's 1598 conquest and settlement of New Mexico.[1] Published in 1610 in Alcalá, Spain, as a book addressed to King Philip III, the poem describes Oñate's journey through New Mexico, concluding with a battle at Acoma in 1599.

In 1610, Spanish authorities established La Villa Real de Santa Fé (the Royal Town of Holy Faith) as Spain's northernmost capital in the New World. (In 1717, the parish church apparently received a new patronal title, Nuestro Padre San Francisco, which resulted in the mistaken belief that Santa Fe's original name was La Villa Real de la Santa Fé de San Francisco de Asís. It seems that the extended name did not fall into use until sometime in the early 1800s, during the Mexican period.) Founded "on the rubble of abandoned Indian settlements"[2] as a Spanish city, Santa Fe represented King Philip III's "seat of the kingdom of New Mexico."[3]

Spanish explorers also traveled seventy miles north to Taos, where, in 1598, they encountered the residents of Taos Pueblo, which historians believe was established sometime between 1300 and 1450. Small groups of Spanish missionaries and colonists settled in the area, sharing an uneasy relationship with the residents of Taos Pueblo, and the town officially was incorporated in 1796 with a Spanish land grant.

During the Spanish Colonial era, families from Spain relocating to the region brought with them traditional songs, ballads, and religious plays. The Spanish settlers also possessed a wealth of folk tales, or *cuentos*— stories that came to New Mexico from Spain, according to acclaimed Albuquerque author Rudolfo Anaya, "but the original tales originated in the subcontinent of India and centuries ago made their way into Persia, then to Europe."[4] Many of these cuentos share similarities with fairy tales from around the world. As settlers repeatedly told these stories in northern New Mexico, the characters took on names and traits associated with Hispano and Pueblo cultures.

Relations between the Spanish explorers and settlers and the Pueblo people already living on the land were hardly peaceful. Attempts by some of the Spanish people to enslave and impose their religion upon the Native Americans resulted in an uprising. After driving the Spanish out of Santa Fe during the Pueblo Revolt of 1680, Pueblo Indians occupied the Palace of the Governors, which had been the seat of Spanish rule since 1610. The Pueblo Indians retained their hold on the Palace until the Spanish mounted a counterattack, reclaiming the city in 1692.

Such dramatic history has provided extensive material over the years for a host of writers working as journalists or penning books of history, fiction, travel writing, poetry, and memoir.

American Hub

After the Spanish reconquered Santa Fe, New Mexico's Spanish Colonial Period lasted for more than a century, until Mexico achieved its independence from Spain in 1821. Unlike Spain, which kept its borders closed, Mexico welcomed trade with the developing United States and New Mexicans began trading with the rest of America. In 1850, following the war between Mexico and America, the United States claimed New Mexico as its own, ushering in the Territorial Period.

New Mexico's population grew even more diverse in the 1800s as newcomers flowed into the dusty brown towns. Rugged mountain men, cowboys, merchants, traders, and pioneer families searching for a new homeland arrived in wagons along the Santa Fe Trail, a trade route stretching 800 miles from Independence, Missouri, to Santa Fe. The trail opened in 1821, the same year Mexico achieved independence from Spain, and visitors poured into Santa Fe as "toward an earthly paradise."[5]

With the start of railway service at the end of the nineteenth century, northern New Mexico took a prominent place on America's evolving map. Speculators, developers, and the merely curious began to flood Santa Fe. The interest heightened when New Mexico officially achieved statehood in 1912.

Early Literary Efforts

The region's complex and compelling history, along with its mesmerizing landscape and golden light, proved irresistible to those with a creative bent. Poetry and prose provided ideal forms for recording individual responses to an entirely new environment, and those who wrote extolled the expansive sky and the unfamiliar cultures sheltered beneath it. No wonder wordsmiths have long been drawn to northern New Mexico.

The first writers of English literature arrived in the early nineteenth century, as Santa Fe poet Alice Corbin Henderson pointed out in her essay surveying New Mexico literature for the 1940 WPA book *New Mexico: A Guide to the Colorful State*. Travel books written by Anglo-Americans and Europeans exploring this part of the country during the Mexican occupation between 1821 and 1846 contained observations reflecting the strong opinions of the writers. One of those travel books greatly appealed to Henderson: *Prose Sketches and Poems, Written in the Western Country*, published in 1834 and written by Albert Pike, the founder of modern Masonry who later fought for the Confederates during the Civil War. Henderson wrote that the book, which grew out of Pike's visit to New Mexico from 1831 to 1833, earned him the distinction of being "the first Anglo-American poet of New Mexico," and his stories and sketches "convey to the reader today the same strangeness of scene which then impressed itself upon the sensitive young poet from the East."[6]

In the wake of the U.S. occupation of New Mexico in 1846, the U.S. Army ordered officers and topographical engineers to prepare reports about the Southwest and then published them as U.S. Senate Executive Documents. Even those men who enlisted in the military became poets once they saw the landscape of the Southwest. Written by Captains

Randolph B. Marcy and Lorenzo Sitgreaves, Lieutenant William Emory, and others, the documents "are anything but dull," Henderson wrote. "Reading them, one is impressed by the high caliber and general cultural background of the young officers who wrote these reports."[7]

W. W. H. Davis, then a U.S. attorney in New Mexico, wrote one of the most famous books of New Mexico's territorial era: *El Gringo; Or, New Mexico and Her People*, published in 1857. His vivid descriptions of life in New Mexico during the 1850s greatly influenced "later writers of the native scene."[8]

The Ramage Press Arrives in New Mexico

The same year that Pike's book was published, the first printing press arrived in New Mexico, paving the way for a new communications era. The wood and iron Ramage hand press traveled on a wagon train from St. Louis, Missouri, along the Santa Fe Trail in 1834, brought by trader Josiah Gregg. A decade after he delivered the Ramage press, Gregg became a famous author with the publication of his *Commerce of the Prairies*. The celebrated two-volume book remains in print primarily because it contains such fascinating detail about the Santa Fe Trail. When the press arrived, it must have looked mighty odd to the citizens of the Republic of Mexico, which was New Mexico's status in 1834. The region had a high percentage of illiterate people in those days and perhaps some people thought the machine would card wool or spin yarn rather than print unfamiliar characters that made little or no sense.

The press Gregg brought to New Mexico probably originated in the Philadelphia shop of Scotland native Adam Ramage. Ramage had devised significant improvements to the handmade wooden press, resulting in an affordable, well-crafted product that, by the early 1800s, had become the most popular press in the country. The particular Ramage press transported to New Mexico was created circa 1820. For more than a decade, it was the sole printing press in New Mexico. Within a century, however, northern New Mexico would become a popular place for private presses producing important works of literature, including *Laughing Horse*, a small satirical magazine that played a big role in America's avant-garde scene.

Padre Antonio José Martínez, an influential and controversial Taos priest, acquired the Ramage press within a year of its arrival and took it to Taos. A politically active Abiquiú native, the priest became the head of the Taos parish in 1826 and fought hard on behalf of the poor, advocating lower taxes and opposing tithing. His stance against certain practices of the Catholic Church made him an enemy of Frenchman Jean Baptiste Lamy, who, as New Mexico's first archbishop, excommunicated Martínez in 1857. More than half a century later, Willa Cather immortalized their enmity in her classic novel *Death Comes for the Archbishop*, published in 1927.

Martínez, who founded New Mexico's first coeducational school in 1826, fully understood the power of the press. Using the Ramage press, he printed textbooks for his school as well as religious and political tracts that included his own writings. The powerful and popular priest, who defied Lamy's censure and continued officiating until his death in 1867, most likely printed the first book in New Mexico—a Spanish spelling primer, *Cuaderno de Ortografi*—which appeared in 1834. His books were tiny by today's standards—four-by-six inches, bound in "muslin, flowered cottons, or leather," and often printed on paper imported from Italy.[9] "They reflect a kind of crude practicality, a frontier craftsmanship that made no attempt to resemble the fine art of printing."[10] Generous with his press, Martínez agreed to loan the Ramage in 1845 to the Mexican government, which published two newspapers from Santa Fe. After 1850, Martínez's press produced *The Laws of the Territory of New Mexico*.

Before the priest's death, the Ramage passed into other hands, indicating, perhaps, that Martínez's feud with Lamy had taken a toll. Seventy years after he died, Taos socialite, art patron, and author Mabel Dodge Luhan—never one to understate her opinions—painted a memorable portrait of the priest in one of her memoirs:

He did not believe in celibacy and a great many women loved him and apparently they all called their offspring Martinez; so his descendants of that name are to be found at all cardinal points of the valley. Magnetic and resolute, when he was excommunicated from the Catholic church he set up a church of his own, taking his whole congregation with him. I have a charcoal drawing of him, made by an admirer from Ranchos de Taos, showing a fierce, bullet-shaped head, intense eyes, and a lower lip that pushes the upper lip up like an iron brace.[11]

Under Martínez's watch, the Ramage press helped advance literacy in New Mexico. Perhaps this mighty priest would not be surprised to learn that within sixty years of his death, scores of literary journals and illustrated books filled with poetry, history, fiction, and more began to roll off hand presses stationed in northern New Mexico. These publications showcased work by Santa Fe and Taos writers and artists and ultimately made their way around the world.

Ben Hur and Billy the Kid in the Land of Poco Tiempo

The writers' colonies in Santa Fe and Taos took off in the 1920s, but other writers began to lay the groundwork for the colonies in the late 1800s. One of the earliest, best-known literary works to emerge from New Mexico, *Ben-Hur: A Tale of the Christ*, appeared in 1880, the same year the railroad arrived in Santa Fe. The novel became an instant best seller and has never gone out of print. Indiana native Lew Wallace set his biblical tale in the Holy Land and may have composed the final chapters in Santa Fe at the Palace of the Governors while serving as New Mexico's territorial governor from 1878 to 1881. If the legend is true, then Wallace sequestered himself in one of the country's oldest buildings, taking time away from his demanding job overseeing a corrupt political system in order to write. There, he "divided his attention between Christian gladiators in Rome and the affairs of Billy the Kid in New Mexico," as Santa Fe poet Alice Corbin Henderson pointed out.[12]

Upon taking office, Wallace received orders from President Rutherford B. Hayes to end the violent Lincoln County Wars. He tried to cut a deal, offering clemency to William Bonney, charged with killing three men, in exchange for his testimony. Bonney, of course, was better known as Billy the Kid, and he fled rather than face prison. One of Wallace's final acts as governor was to sign the outlaw's warrant before leaving the territory for good. In 1881, under Wallace's orders, Sheriff Pat F. Garrett shot and killed the Kid.

Perhaps taking a cue from Wallace and the runaway success of *Ben Hur*, Garrett wrote the *Authentic Life of Billy the Kid*, published just two years later. Since then, many writers have published works of fiction and fact about one of the Wild West's most famous outlaws, including speculation that he escaped Garrett's gunshots and lived to a ripe old age.

When *Ben Hur* was published, Wallace was on leave from his duties as governor of the New Mexico Territory, which may explain why his book sold so well—he must have had time for promotion and marketing. The plot of his famous novel had no connection to New Mexico, except, perhaps, that it was set in a desert not unlike northern New Mexico's high and dry plateau. Wallace disliked the disorder that marked New Mexico's politics: "All calculations based on our experiences elsewhere fail in New Mexico," he famously wrote in an April 29, 1881 letter sent to his wife in their native Indiana, where she, also unhappy with New Mexico life, was waiting for his term as territorial governor to end.[13]

Susan E. Wallace felt compelled by her own Southwest experience to chronicle her impressions of New Mexico life and history. The descriptive letters she wrote for a newspaper back East were published in 1888 in the nonfiction book *The Land of the Pueblos*. She also wrote other works of nonfiction, fiction, and poetry, some of which her husband illustrated.

Charles Lummis, a journalist, folklorist, pioneer photographer, and editor of the *Daily Times* in Los Angeles, made important contributions to the canon of early literature, planting the seeds of a fertile literary movement in northern New Mexico. Lummis traveled to the territory after suffering a stroke in Los Angeles in 1887. Growing up in Massachusetts, he had left Harvard without completing his degree to become a freelance writer and ardent adventurer. In the Southwest, he explored the land and its peoples on horseback, joining archaeological expeditions. His 1893 classic nonfiction book *The Land of Poco Tiempo* paid tribute to the laid-back lifestyle he encountered in New Mexico, where people never hurried and everything took its own time. His interpretation of the Spanish phrase *Poco tiempo* as "pretty soon" offered an apt description of the land where writers rarely rushed to meet deadlines. Lummis was all too familiar with deadlines. His work as a journalist and author reached the masses and undoubtedly lured tourists, especially when he extolled Taos Pueblo as "The American Pyramids" and New Mexico as "the Great American Mystery" in *Land of Poco Tiempo*.[14]

Lummis served for a time as mentor to Mary Austin, a major figure of the Santa Fe writers' colony and a prolific author of novels, nonfiction books, essays, articles, and several plays. Austin must have taken a cue or two from his writings. After her initial encounters with the Native American cultures and landscape of the Southwest, she wrote two nonfiction books—the 1903 *Land of Little Rain*, about California, and the 1924 *Land of Journey's Ending*, about New Mexico and Arizona. Both titles send a clear nod to Lummis's classic, *Land of Poco Tiempo*. Such synergy was not unusual in the Santa Fe and Taos colonies, where authors united to fight for an array of causes, from Indian rights to the preservation and promotion of traditional art and culture.

Legendary Literary Gatherings

The writers and artists of this era banded together frequently, organizing projects and programs as often as they threw together luncheons and dinner parties at each other's houses. Teas were popular too, mainly because they were "often thinly disguised Prohibition cocktail parties" that honored visiting literary lions such as Vachel Lindsay in 1929, Thornton Wilder in 1933 and 1934, and Edna Ferber in 1935.[15] When venerated poet Robert Frost visited Santa Fe on August 5, 1935, speaking to more than 200 guests at the New Mexico Museum auditorium in an event sponsored by the influential Writers' Editions group, playwright and poet Lynn Riggs gave tribute, praising Frost for "the compassionate, stirring things he says of the gracious earth and its people."[16] Later, however, during an honorary luncheon at Witter Bynner's house, the Santa Fe poet became sufficiently irate about something Frost said, and Bynner's anger may have chased the prestigious Pulitzer Prize–winning poet from Santa Fe for good. That didn't deter these writers, however, from their legendary literary gatherings, which often lasted into the early morning hours.

The writers and artists dined together in local restaurants too, with lively meals in La Fonda's Harvey House dining room and on its handsome Spanish-style porch. George Park's New Mexico Cafe, located at 126 San Francisco Street next to what then was called The Paris Theatre, served "Real Chinese dishes that have won praise from visiting orientalists, and the finest of American steaks and chops," according to an old advertisement.[17] Witter Bynner, who traveled extensively through the Far East, wrote a little poem for the ad, titled "The New Mexico Cafe":

If you choose wise as a diner,
You are sure to find no dinner finer
Than the Parks can prepare,
Whether U.S.A. fare
Or the properest viands from Chiner.[18]

Later, noteworthy writers chronicled the humor and hardships of life in the Southwest. Oliver La Farge, for instance—recipient of a Pulitzer Prize for his 1929 Navajo love story *Laughing Boy*—captured the amusing and often frustrating aspects of life in a Southwestern town struggling to maintain its identity as hordes of artists, cosmopolitans, and other outsiders descended to visit and often settled permanently. La Farge's columns about Santa Fe life appeared in the local newspaper and the *New Yorker*, reaching audiences near and far. "Once everyone in the United States knows what New Mexico is like, everyone will come here, and we of New Mexico, in turn, to save our lives, can pull up stakes and take over New England," he wrote with characteristic humor in one of his columns for the *Santa Fe New Mexican*.[19]

Mural for the Laboratory of Anthropology by William Lumpkin. Photo by T. Parkhust. Courtesy Palace of the Governors (MNM/DCA). Negative no. 74062.

Other writers also wielded their pens in an attempt to save Santa Fe's historic charm from the onslaught of development. In the 1930s, La Farge joined forces with noted printer, poet, and essayist Willard "Spud" Johnson and poet Alice Corbin Henderson to produce the *Santa Fe Plaza: A Weekly News Magazine of Old Santa Fe*, a well-written but "short-lived" publication devoted to the "survival of the village under the press of Cosmopolis."[20]

As the twentieth century unfolded, northern New Mexico became home to a number of established and emerging writers, drawn to the state because the natural and cultural environments enhanced their work. The colonies they created reached their peaks during the 1920s and 1930s, but activity began as early as 1916 in Santa Fe and 1917 in Taos, with the arrival of two strong-willed, independent women: poet Alice Corbin Henderson in Santa Fe and heiress, arts patron, and author Mabel Dodge Luhan in Taos.

PART ONE

In Santa Fe

You will find the more successful or the handsome-though-poor-ones at the smart tea-parties and the scornful young poets, the more determinedly "modern" painters, and the "proletarian" artists and writers renting a plumbingless mud house at ten dollars a month, with a yellow rosebush beside the well or plum-trees along the irrigation ditch, while the fashionable portrait-painter, the writer of best-sellers, or the blue-stocking may have the house next door, which has three bathrooms and a Spanish garden, and rents for two hundred dollars. . . . Chummy, that's the word for Santa Fe social life!

—Spud Johnson writing in *Vogue*,
October 15, 1936

Alice Corbin Henderson and William Penhallow Henderson,
1932. Photo by Will Connell. Courtesy Palace
of the Governors (MNM/DCA). Neg. no. 59757.

CHAPTER TWO

Alice Corbin Henderson

In Search of Health

WHO WERE THESE writers and why did they seek refuge in the extremely isolated northern New Mexico country, the land of mañana, where nothing was so important that it couldn't happen tomorrow, or, even better, the day after that? The answers are numerous, but a good place to start is the hope for health.

Santa Fe's Sunmount Sanatorium, run by Dr. Frank Mera, became a popular spot for those suffering from tuberculosis in the early part of the twentieth century. The facility held the best reputation among the forty or so sanatoriums then operating across New Mexico.[1] Built on the lower flank of Sun Mountain about a mile and a half from the Santa Fe plaza, it offered patients a solid treatment of rest, healthy food, and a dry climate. Accommodations included cabins with sleeping porches where patients could breathe a constant supply of fresh air. From numerous terraces and balconies, magnificent views of mesas and mountains could soothe and inspire the spirit.

Poet Alice Corbin Henderson was the first member of the Santa Fe writers' colony group to settle in Santa Fe, and Sunmount was the reason. Henderson had secured a prominent place in the Chicago poetry scene as associate editor of *Poetry*, invited by the magazine's founder Harriet Monroe to take the position when the magazine launched in

1912. She had also published two books of poetry, married artist William Penhallow Henderson, and become a mother. Then tuberculosis threatened to destroy everything she had accomplished. Informing her that she would not live for more than a year, her doctor prescribed a stay at Sunmount.

Traveling to New Mexico by train in March 1916, with her husband and their nine-year-old daughter, Alice, (known as Little Alice), Henderson must have been terrified facing what she thought was certain death. Later she recorded what was running through her mind as she voyaged into an unknown country: "I had been thrown out into the desert to die, like a piece of old scrap-iron, or a rusty Ford."[2] Instead of death, however, she discovered a brand new life. She felt so inspired by the unfamiliar land and cultures she encountered that she invited friends and colleagues from Chicago and elsewhere to visit so they, too, could share the experience.

A letter Henderson sent on March 28, 1916, to poet Carl Sandburg, whose career she helped launch by publishing his work in *Poetry*, might well be the reason one of America's greatest twentieth-century poets visited Santa Fe several times during the 1920s and 1930s. Henderson rhapsodized about the vistas from her cottage that took in the "sand-combed valley to the west," the "mesas rising out of it," and the "snow-capped mountains of the Sangre de Cristo range."[3] Sandburg's return letter of April 2 offered an eloquent testimony to what New Mexico had done to Henderson. He was, he told her, replying to those who asked about her well-being with the comment that she had "slipped into quiet, pearl-walled caves of quiet, and was learning new values of dream."[4] Sandburg, the recipient of two Pulitzer prizes, later visited Santa Fe, serenading guests with folk songs as he played guitar at a reception Henderson held in his honor.

Sandburg was right on the mark, for Henderson had undoubtedly renewed her sense of wonder. The place she believed would be a "desolate exile" instead astounded her as "a new world of beauty."[5] Other writers she soon would meet enthusiastically shared her point of view.

Starting the Santa Fe Colony

Henderson overcame her illness and in the process, her quick, bright wit brought a literary light to Sunmount, which fit well with the sanatorium's mission to highlight art and culture in its program. Dr. Frank Mera, the head of the sanatorium, encouraged his patients to create poetry and perform theater. He also invited writers, artists, and archaeologists to present guest lectures to patients. Henderson, a patient during her first year in Santa Fe and then again in 1921, had many of her poet friends visit her at Sunmount.

From 1917 to 1923, the Henderson family took up residence down the road from Sunmount in a small adobe house on what was then called Telegraph Road. (In keeping with her desire to celebrate traditional culture, Henderson convinced city authorities to officially change Telegraph Road's name back to its original Spanish name, Camino del Monte Sol, or Road of the Sun Mountain, which remains in use today.) In 1924, Henderson's husband built the family a larger home nearby, in the same area where other artists who had recently settled in Santa Fe built their homes and studios. William Penhallow Henderson, an acclaimed architect of Santa Fe Style, also designed an elegant adobe on Garcia Street that now houses the School of American Research as well as the Wheelwright Museum building on Museum Hill.

The Hendersons turned their family home into a central gathering spot for the growing group of writers, artists, and intellectuals who settled in Santa Fe, as well as for those whose curiosity brought them to visit. By the mid-1920s, the Henderson house had become the weekly meeting place for a group of Santa Fe poets that included Witter Bynner, Haniel Long, Spud Johnson, and poet and playwright Lynn Riggs. The group, as Johnson explained, "seemed to lapse so often into a Rabelaisian mood, that soon we were referring to ourselves as the Rabelais Club, which was quickly altered, since that sounded much too stodgy, to the simple informality of the 'The Rabble.'"[6] The group took its name from sixteenth-century French writer François Rabelais, known for his humorous social and political satire.

Living in Santa Fe, Henderson and her family became absorbed in an entirely different lifestyle from the one they had known in Chicago. American Studies scholar and author Lois Palken Rudnick described it: "They learned the daily rhythms determined by sun and rainfall, had heating wood delivered by burros, watched the earth behind their small adobe serve as a floor for the threshing of wheat, listened to men and women telling tales and singing folk songs, and participated in weddings, christenings, festivals, and wakes."[7]

The slow pace, connected to the cycles of the seasons, returned Henderson to good health and resulted in a new style of writing that celebrated the simplicity of life in northern New Mexico. As Rudnick pointed out, "If she came increasingly to value Indian and Hispano folkways and folk arts during her years in Santa Fe, it was because their religious and aesthetic expressions were directly related to what she came to believe were the most important aspects of human life—loving, preparing food, rejoicing in the harvest, story-telling, caring for the sick, and respecting the old."[8]

Red Earth

In 1920, Henderson published *Red Earth: Poems of New Mexico*, a significant collection of her poetry that included work first published in *Poetry* magazine. In Rudnick's introduction to the 2003 reissue of *Red Earth*, she wrote that Henderson's book instantly took an important place in modern American poetry "both because of its aesthetic power and because the poems selected for it made an important contribution to the culture wars that were occurring over the formation of the modern poetry canon in the early twentieth century."[9]

In Santa Fe, Henderson found new ways to write. In Chicago, she had joined the Imagist school, conceived in 1912 by Ezra Pound as a reaction, in part, to Romanticism and conventional verse forms. Imagist poets stressed the importance of clear, precise language to describe an exact visual image in free verse. Yet now, in this unfamiliar land she inhabited, Henderson felt free to combine elements of the Imagist school with the rhythms she discovered in New Mexico, including Hispano and Native American folk songs. Her New Mexico poetry contained a rich tapestry of "voices, forms and styles" that introduced Americans to strong notions of "cultural pluralism and environmental awareness."[10]

The untitled poem below, which Henderson placed at the front of *Red Earth*, signaled to readers that they were entering an unfamiliar and powerful land of space and silences, which greatly contrasted with the noisy and hectic pace of city space. As Rudnick pointed out, the poem aptly illustrates Henderson's grasp of the world she now inhabited, where the red earth worked by Pueblo potters lay light years away from Europe's bloody battlegrounds of World War I.[11]

After the roar, after the fierce modern music
Of rivets and hammers and trams,
After the shout of the giant,
Youthful and brawling and strong
Building the cities of men,
Here is the desert of silence,
Blinking and blind in the sun—
An old, old woman who mumbles her beads
And crumbles to stone.[12]

Connecting with Community

Henderson eagerly joined the Santa Fe and Taos community of writers who banded together to defeat the Bursum Bill. Introduced in the U.S. Congress in 1922, the legislation outraged people across the country because it gave Hispanos and Anglos the right to own land that belonged to Pueblo Indians. Henderson stepped into the fray, signing her name to the national "Artists and Writers Protest" and writing articles for the *Nation* and the *New Republic* magazines.[13] (See chapter 7 for more information on the Bursum Bill.) After the bill's defeat, Henderson continued to work on behalf of Pueblo Indians and their art forms as a member of the New Mexico Association on Indian Affairs. (The group later changed its name to the Southwestern Association on Indian Affairs, and organizes the annual Santa Fe Indian Market, which now attracts an estimated 100,000 visitors from around the world.)

Henderson took an active role in promoting New Mexico in numerous other ways. She compiled the 1928 groundbreaking book *The Turquoise Trail, An Anthology of New Mexico Poetry*, filled with the verse of thirty-seven contributors who drew inspiration from New Mexico. The anthology demonstrated that Native American culture and the New Mexico landscape had undeniably influenced a host of acclaimed authors now living in the state, including Mary Austin, Witter Bynner, D. H. Lawrence, Mabel Dodge Luhan, and Henderson. In her preface to the anthology, Henderson paid tribute to the connections between two diverse cultures: "On the common ground of poetry, indeed, the living Indian poets and the Anglo-American poets of New Mexico now meet in friendly contact; and the influence of this primitive verse and thought on the later poets is obvious."[14]

Furthering the spirit of community that brought the writers in Santa Fe together as a colony, Henderson helped organize the Poets' Roundups, a series of poetry readings inspired by rodeo events that writers hosted in their gardens from 1930 to 1939 to raise funds for the New Mexico Association on Indian Affairs. The readers, including Mary Austin, Witter Bynner, and Haniel Long, made sure the events were entertaining. "At the annual spectacles local and visiting poets, resplendent in bandanas and blue jeans, would dash out of cardboard chutes to recite their works for appreciative listeners."[15]

Writers' Editions and the Rydal Press

Henderson also joined Santa Fe writer Raymond Otis and poets Haniel Long and Peggy Pond Church as charter members of Writers' Editions, a cooperative publishing venture of Santa Fe and Taos writers launched in the mid-1930s. (For more information on Church, see chapter 11; for more information on Otis and Long, see chapter 12.) Writers' Editions marked a new and highly successful chapter in New Mexico book publishing with the arrival of Walter Lippincott Goodwin Jr. in Santa Fe in 1933. Goodwin, a talented printer and publisher who came from a wealthy family in Rydal, Pennsylvania, was production manager and book designer at the J. B. Lippincott publishing house. By 1930, he had established the Rydal Press, a private venture in Pennsylvania that produced high-quality art books as well as an imprint, Arrow Editions, devoted to limited-edition books created by his circle of New York friends. When he received an invitation from the Writers' Editions founders to work in Santa Fe, Goodwin promptly accepted, excited by the opportunity to create high-quality regionalist books. Hauling his printing machinery halfway across the country, Goodwin set up shop north of Santa Fe in Tesuque village and began to print exceptional, award-winning books. Rydal Press soon had its own printer's mark— a small saint cradling two printer's inking balls between his hands— drafted by illustrator and type inventor Warren Chappell.

The Writers' Editions' credo, which appeared on most of its books, called for regional publication to "foster the growth of American literature."[16] The group's seventeen publications reflected the varied voices of the region. In 1933, for instance, Writers' Editions published three poetry books: Henderson's *The Sun Turns West*, containing work from 1915 to 1932; Haniel Long's *Atlantides*; and Peggy Pond Church's *Foretaste*. John Gould Fletcher's 1935 poetry collection *XXIV Elegies*, and *Frijoles Canyon Pictographs*, a 1939 book of Santa Fe artist Gustave Baumann's woodblock prints of ancient Native American cave drawings, ended up on the prestigious American Institute of Graphic Arts' Fifty Books of the Year list.

Goodwin's press achieved such success that by 1937, he expanded his business and moved it to 998 Canyon Road in Santa Fe. Within two years, though, Writers' Editions began to wane, due in part to the onset of World War II and the 1938 death of one of its founders, Otis. Goodwin sold Rydal Press in 1941 and left New Mexico in 1946, only to return later to operate a quarter horse ranch in Pojoaque, up the road from his original business spot in Tesuque. The Rydal Press stayed in business until 1976, printing eighty or so books, but eventually its focus became commercial rather than literary. Clark Kimball revived the Rydal Press in the 1980s as a private Santa Fe publishing venture, but that, too, eventually folded.[17]

Connecting with New Mexico Culture

Even during Writers' Editions' heyday, Henderson still found time to work on an array of diverse projects. Her interest in eclectic songs resulted in several books, including *Brothers of the Light: The Penitentes of the Southwest*, a collection of Spanish religious songs sung by the Penitentes, a secretive group of Hispano Catholic men. Published in 1937 with illustrations by Henderson's husband, the book also contained information about the group's history and ritual ceremonies.

Henderson also contributed to *New Mexico: A Guide to the Colorful State*, one of a series of travel guides to American states launched by the Works Progress Administration to increase tourism. The book took longer to complete than planned and, when finally published in 1940, it contained Henderson's informative essay on New Mexico literature. The essay began with the acknowledgment that New Mexico's literary tradition "begins with orally transmitted myths, legends, and rituals of the Indians who were native to the soil when the Spaniards came," and that the first written books were "the old Spanish chronicles of exploration and conquest. These basic sources of history rank among the great original adventure books of the world."[18] Rudnick pointed out that when Henderson made this assertion, hardly anyone had thought to make the same connections between literature and Native American storytelling.[19]

To further her interest in Native American art and culture, Henderson agreed to serve as the first curator of the Museum of Navaho Ceremonial Art, housed in a building designed by her husband. Mary Cabot Wheelwright, a wealthy Bostonian who spent time living in northern New Mexico, established the museum in 1937. (The museum later changed its name to the Wheelwright Museum of the American Indian.)

Henderson's pivotal role in the Santa Fe literary colony meant that she kept in close contact with the writers of the Taos literary colony. Although Mabel Dodge Luhan clearly presided over the group in Taos and could often be difficult, she and Henderson worked together on issues such as the defeat of the Bursum Bill. Whether they desired it or not, their relationship grew even closer with the marriage of Henderson's daughter, Alice, at age fifteen, to Luhan's only child, John Evans, her son by her first husband. The marriage ultimately ended in divorce, but the couple's three daughters spent time in both Santa Fe and Taos, connecting the two families through history.

A Farewell Tribute

Henderson's husband died of a heart attack in 1943, but she, who had been told she would die within a year in 1916, lived until July 18, 1949. A few months before her death, Henderson's friends and colleagues paid tribute to her invaluable role as a poet, editor, and activist in Santa Fe with a special edition of *New Mexico Quarterly Review*, published by the University of New Mexico. Edited by Santa Fe poet Witter Bynner and Santa Fe author Oliver La Farge, the commemorative edition contained glowing accounts of her friendship and professional stature in the community. Bynner may have put it best, in his essay "Alice and I," when he wrote that during "that golden period of American poetry, her vivid, sympathetic spirit meant much more to most of the poets who made it golden, as it has meant much to all of us who have encountered her in poetry or in life."[20]

CHAPTER THREE

Witter Bynner

ONE OF THE POETS Alice Corbin Henderson invited to visit Santa Fe also became an important and permanent member of the literary community. When Witter Bynner first arrived in Santa Fe on February 20, 1922, to give a lecture, an attack of influenza landed him in Sunmount for a brief cure. During his stay, he found Santa Fe's culture, landscape, and community of writers so alluring that he made it his home for the rest of his life. Among the mountains and mesas of New Mexico, Bynner felt he could accurately measure his own self-worth, writing that the "Southwestern landscape, more than any other in North America, reduces vainglory in a man and enforces his exact, or at least his reasonable, importance. It is at once a humbling and an ennobling landscape."[1]

One Poet's Beginnings

A poet and graduate of Harvard, Bynner launched his career in New York as an editor of *McClure's Magazine*. He worked for the influential literary and political publication from 1902 to 1906 and brought several important writers into its pages, including short story author William Sydney Porter, better known as O. Henry. Well before Bynner first set foot in Santa Fe, he had a run-in with another writer whose visit to

Witter Bynner (left) with Frieda and D. H. Lawrence, outside Bynner's house, 1922 or 1923. Courtesy The Witter Bynner Foundation for Poetry.

Santa Fe proved fateful—Willa Cather, who also worked as an editor and writer at *McClure's*. According to Bynner's biographer, James Kraft, magazine publisher S. S. McClure asked Bynner to edit one of Cather's stories. When Cather expressed anger at Bynner's changes, McClure vehemently denied having any role in the affair. Bynner continued to edit other writers' work, so this encounter with Cather presumably had little or no input to his decision to leave the magazine in 1906, especially since he told others that he hoped to devote more time to his own writing. He took up residence with friends in Cornish, New Hampshire, a summer community for wealthy New Yorkers and Bostonians and an enclave for artists, where he worked on his first book, *An Ode to Harvard and Other Poems*, which appeared in 1907. A second book of poems, *The New World*, followed in 1915. Both books "show Bynner reaching out for ideas that could establish order in his personal and poetic worlds," Kraft wrote.[3] *Ode* lyrically explored such traditional themes as "nature, youth, beauty and death," which surfaced repeatedly in Bynner's work throughout his life.[4] *The New World* offered "a Whitmanesque song in praise of the New America" that reflected

"Bynner's growing awareness of the changing America that was taking shape around him, the new order he saw coming into existence as the vast immigrant population took its place."[5]

The Spectra Hoax

In 1916, when Bynner and a friend launched the Spectra Hoax, one of the great literary ruses of the twentieth century, Bynner was considered "one of the bright young names" in American literature.[6] He ranked equally with his contemporaries, American poets Amy Lowell, Carl Sandburg, Vachel Lindsay, and Edna St. Vincent Millay, to whom he was briefly engaged. (Bynner, a homosexual, established a close friendship with Millay. She accepted his proposal in 1921, but it's unlikely that either of them took the engagement seriously.[7]) Despite his reputation, or perhaps because of it, Bynner had grown tired of the numerous schools of poetry that had cropped up in recent years. He enlisted the help of his good friend and Harvard classmate, poet and lawyer Arthur Davison Ficke, to demonstrate how easy it was to create a trend in poetry and probably also to play with his skills in a new way. Together, they invented the school of Spectrism, "which tried to see the spectre in our life and capture the varied light of the spectrum."[8] The theory "was just convincing enough to be believable in a day when everyone was trying the new and was afraid of rejecting it."[9] Creating fictitious personas that hailed from Pittsburgh and boasted European backgrounds, Bynner took the name of Emanuel Morgan and Ficke took the name of Anne Knish.

Although Bynner and Ficke intended their Spectra poetry to be humorous, the verse they wrote was good enough for influential magazines to publish it and top critics of the day to praise it. When it was finally exposed a few years after it started, the hoax hurt Bynner's reputation. Expressing outrage that their contemporaries would undertake such a parody, many of the country's leading poets turned against Bynner and Ficke. By inventing the Spectra Hoax, Bynner "created great uncertainty about himself and his poetry among contemporary poets and critics."[10] Yet at the same time, Kraft pointed out, the experiment unlocked a new style of writing in Bynner.

Asian Influences

Perhaps the greatest influence to liberate Bynner's writing style came from the time he spent in Asia. He traveled in China and Japan for four months in 1917, then returned to China from June 1920 until April 1921. Before his second trip to China, he taught a poetry class at the University of California at Berkeley, where he met Kiang Kang-hu, a Chinese scholar forced to leave his native country because of his politics. Working together, the pair translated three hundred T'ang poems for *Jade Mountain*, an anthology they took eight years to complete. Published in 1929, the book "has always been popular and is a considerable achievement in its accurate and sensitive rendering of poems thought of as Chinese classics and very difficult to translate," Kraft wrote.[11] Many of the Chinese poems recounted intense emotional experiences with plain yet potent language, a style that greatly inspired Bynner in his own work. Here, for example, is a translation of "In the Quiet Night," a poem by T'ang poet Li Po:

> So bright a gleam on the foot of my bed—
> Could there have been a frost already?
> Lifting myself to look, I found that it was moonlight.
> Sinking back again, I thought suddenly of home.[12]

The Way of Life According to Laotzu: An American Version proved to be the most successful work that emerged from Bynner's love affair with Asia. His lyrical translation, based on existing English translations of the classic work by the founder of Taoism, was published in 1944 by the John Day Company. It became Bynner's most popular book, though ironically his regular publisher, Alfred A. Knopf, rejected it on the grounds that it would not sell well. Bynner sent the manuscript to a college friend who owned the John Day Company and who agreed to publish it. The book's subtitle reveals that Bynner hoped modern American readers would find inspiration in his translation of a work that portrays an alternative to warfare, especially since his book was published during World War II. "In this, he succeeded admirably," Kraft wrote.[13] The book remains in print today, a testament to Bynner's talent through translation to reach across the ages and bring an ancient text to life so that it could touch contemporary readers.

While teaching at Berkeley, Bynner came under fire from community civic leaders for supporting the release of conscientious objectors to World War I from prison. He also got in trouble for serving alcohol to freshman and drinking too much of it himself at a campus event. The negative publicity compelled him to leave Berkeley, a place he initially considered calling home. Understandably, he then went to China for his second trip to Asia and when he returned to the United States, he decided to organize a lecture tour of the Southwest.

The tour took place in 1922 and included Santa Fe, primarily because of Alice Corbin Henderson, who first met Bynner in 1916 in Chicago. Bynner had been there to present a lecture on contemporary American poetry, before his Spectra school had been exposed as a hoax. During a question-and-answer period following the lecture, Henderson, a proponent of Imagism, challenged Bynner's fundamental statement that Spectra verse was superior to Imagist verse because it rejected an intellectual approach to the subject, allowing the inner consciousness to select images instead. Bynner responded to Henderson by admitting that he had adopted a "brash platform" and was taking Spectrism too seriously. He did not, however, reveal his ruse. A "sharp but friendly interchange" between Bynner and Henderson followed.[14]

This initial encounter resulted in Henderson's invitation to Bynner to visit her studio in Chicago. There he met her daughter, Alice, and husband, William Penhallow Henderson. After leaving Chicago, Bynner stayed in touch with the family. He knew they settled in Santa Fe so that Henderson could receive treatment for tuberculosis. Henderson's offer to visit Santa Fe arrived at the right time. The town's growing reputation as a center for writers and artists held great appeal for Bynner, who had just returned from his second trip to China and was living in a New York hotel. His constant traveling seemed "almost as if these trips had become a search for a place he could remain."[15] In the Southwest, he would finally find that desired home.

Settling in Santa Fe

When Bynner got to Santa Fe, Henderson was at Sunmount for her tuberculosis treatment. In his essay "Alice and I," Bynner details sanatorium life in 1922:

Alice Corbin's room, perhaps purposely, was opposite the doctor's office. She was not only a bed-patient but under strict watch as to rest and diet. Doctors, nurses, servants, and patients were all, in those years, easy comrades and so were such guests as lived long enough in the haphazard hotel section to become fellow Santa Feans. Waitresses would bring coffee for groups in this or that private room instead of serving it at this or that table in the long dining hall. Later Alice brewed her own coffee, and we would gather nightly in her room for gay, swift talk and forbidden cigarettes. Now and then we would enjoy in our coffee cups a fill or two of Taos Lightning, that fiery corn whiskey which we keg-rolled in the backs of our cars.[16]

After delivering his lecture, "The Heart of China," which was warmly received by Santa Fe residents, and recovering from the flu, Bynner decided to settle in Santa Fe. He appreciated the similarities shared by the mountainous landscapes, contoured houses, and people of Peking with the adobe homes, Sangre de Cristo Mountains, and Pueblo Indians of northern New Mexico, believing that the Pueblo people resembled the Chinese in manner and characteristics.[17] A few years after arriving in Santa Fe, Bynner wrote descriptively about the Pueblo people: "And round about the landscape, in their snug, earthen pueblos, were Indians, guarding the dignity of their race and instinctively living the beauty of their religion and their art, as they had been doing for hundreds of years."[18]

Santa Fe's wealth of culture and history prompted Bynner to become an active member of the literary and art communities, which worked hard to preserve Native American and Hispano art forms and New Mexico history. To that end, he became an active supporter of the Santa Fe Fiesta, which paid tribute to the Spanish reconquest of Santa Fe following the 1680 Pueblo Revolt. Launched in 1712 as an annual event that soon stopped being held each year, the fiesta quickly faded from history until the mid-1920s, when the artists and writers of Santa Fe helped reinvigorate it with new activities, including a parade. The revitalized fiesta aimed at celebrating more than just Spanish history, featuring tributes to Santa Fe's past and present from Pueblo and Anglo cultures as well. For years, Bynner led the parade dressed in hilarious costumes with Dolly Sloan, wife of the prominent painter John Sloan, who spent time in Santa Fe. One year, Bynner paraded as an infant, swaddled in diapers and carrying a giant baby bottle filled with alcohol.

Bynner found ample reason to stay in Santa Fe in the busy social life of the writers and artists, who hosted teas, readings, parties, and other events on a regular basis. Purchasing a small adobe on Buena Vista Street, he added room after room over the years. By the time he died there on June 1, 1968, his residence had become a true rambling adobe, filled with Native American rugs, Spanish Colonial folk art, and art from Asia. He financed a second story, built in the 1920s, by selling three manuscripts of O. Henry stories, given to him by the author to repay a loan. Naturally, Bynner dubbed the new addition the O. Henry Story. A popular host who loved to entertain, Bynner threw legendary parties in his handsome home attended by writers, artists, musicians, composers, actors, and other noteworthy people who lived in the region or passed through on visits. One of his famous guests, poet Robert Frost, stayed only briefly, but his visit has become notorious.

A Cold Encounter

When Frost trekked to Santa Fe in 1935 for a speaking engagement he was, by then, considered one of America's great poets. Perhaps Bynner's failure to achieve the same fame explains why he felt compelled to pour a glass of beer on Frost's head during a luncheon at his house. Bynner later wrote Frost an apology stating that the incident was a joke that had "misfired," but the event, according to his biographer Kraft, "was a lame attempt to cover his anger."[19]

Bynner's relationships with Santa Fe poets fared better. Not long after arriving in New Mexico, he attended Pueblo ceremonial dances with the Hendersons, which he described in his poetry. Viewing the dances was a serious endeavor, and Bynner once wrote that he and his companions "liked to watch singly and to absorb the dances, or to be absorbed by them, rather than to make them the social occasions they are now."[20] He did, however, thoroughly enjoy social occasions, and when people gathered in his home and elsewhere, guests relinquished the spotlight to his sparkling conversation filled with wit and knowledge. That quick wit could cut someone who crossed him, but he had a playful side too. When, for instance, journalist Elizabeth Shepley Sergeant wrote a 1934 article for the *Saturday Review of Literature*

"D. H. Lawrence," pen and ink drawing by Witter Bynner
from *Laughing Horse*, no. 13 (1926).
Courtesy Gerald Peters Gallery Bookstore.

chronicling life in Santa Fe, she described her mud house made out of
adobe bricks, prompting Bynner and other Santa Fe writers and artists
to good-naturedly begin calling themselves "mud-hut nuts."

Being Gay in Santa Fe

Bynner's homosexuality, for the most part, was not controversial in
Santa Fe. As one character exclaims in *Fire in the Night*—a 1934 roman
à clef set in Santa Fe by Santa Fe writer Raymond Otis—"nobody gives
much of a damn what other people do."[21] Once the writers and artists

had established themselves, a sense of bohemianism reigned. Hence when budding poet, journalist, and magazine editor Spud Johnson arrived in Santa Fe in 1922, working as Bynner's secretary and living with him as a lover, few eyebrows were raised. Johnson and Bynner met at the University of California, Berkeley, where Johnson took classes and Bynner taught. Johnson was one of three founders of *Laughing Horse*, a small, satirical magazine that he relocated to Santa Fe after leaving Berkeley. (He fled the campus following a furor over the magazine's publication of a book review by D. H. Lawrence containing language university officials thought should have been censored.) Bynner published numerous poems and articles in *Laughing Horse*, including some of the Spectra poems he wrote using the pseudonym Emanuel Morgan. (See chapter 10 for more information about *Laughing Horse*.)

In Santa Fe, Bynner and Johnson became "lovers and friends, but also father and son, teacher and student," according to Kraft.[22] The relationship didn't last for several reasons cited by the biographers of both men. Kraft explained that because Spud was too "indecisive" and unwilling to commit himself to a mentor, Bynner was ready to let him go.[23] Both Kraft and Sharyn Udall, author of *Spud Johnson & Laughing Horse*, made it clear that Mabel Dodge Luhan, the domineering force behind the Taos writers' colony, had a hand in the break-up as well. When Bynner and Johnson accompanied D. H. Lawrence and his wife, Frieda, on a trip through Mexico in 1923 without inviting Luhan to accompany them, her desire to control events and people got the better of her. She exacted revenge for being left out of the Mexico trip by hiring Johnson to be her secretary and taking him up to Taos, where he settled in an adobe house and became a literary personality. Presumably, working for Luhan demanded more than serving as Bynner's secretary, as she attempted to exert her dominating will over everybody who entered her circle.

Complications with Compadres

For his part, Bynner got back at Luhan by authoring *Cake: An Indulgence*, a 1926 verse play that satirized Luhan by depicting a wealthy woman's attempt to cure her boredom by experimenting with religion, alcohol, sex, and, as a final resort, cake. A piece of absurd theater, the play "portrays modern woman as emasculator, goddess of wealth, and deceiver of both men and herself, but very much her own mistress/master," Kraft wrote, adding that Bynner regarded The Lady in *Cake* as "liberated, free to discover her character and her place in the world." The play "is principally an attack on the materialism and destructiveness of American society and not on the American female."[24] Nonetheless, many people felt the play attacked her, including Luhan, though she claimed never to have read it.

Cake may be the principal reason why the relationship between Luhan and Bynner stayed sour until 1950, when they both attended a Thanksgiving dinner at the home of Millicent Rogers, an oil heiress and arts patron who had a home in Taos. When Bynner arrived, Luhan sat alone in a separate room. According to Mabel's biographer, Lois Palken Rudnick, Bynner must have felt the rivalry had endured long enough and he approached Mabel. The two had a long talk, ostensibly ending their feud. Five years later, when *Cake* was performed in Taos, Bynner invited Luhan to attend but she declined, sending him a note that she wished him to be the focus of the evening instead of her. Bynner wrote her one final letter a month later, thanking her for sending him a cigarette case and a playful note that offered what Rudnick called "a gently ironic commentary on their relationship." In his letter, Bynner expressed thanks for the case and suggested they "continue the flirting."[25] Luhan lived until 1962 and Bynner until 1968, but the two never saw each other or communicated again.

Bynner had a complicated relationship with D. H. Lawrence as well. In his 1951 memoir, *Journey with Genius: Recollections and Reflections Concerning the D. H. Lawrences*, Bynner recounts his travels during 1923 through Mexico with Spud Johnson and D. H. and Frieda Lawrence. Bynner's book contains criticism as well as praise for Lawrence. "Yes, Lawrence was generous, more than generous," Bynner wrote. "But he could not rid his mind of the theory that he did not love people and did not want people to love him."[26] Bynner grew weary of Lawrence's sudden outbursts, but he could see through the bouts of juvenile behavior to the flashes of brilliance: "In spite or perhaps because of his poutings and foot stampings, his semitragic impatience with burdens pettier than those of Atlas, despite the fact that he was born without divine laughter and could never attain it, what a good time he finally had, on a beautiful earth, in an eternity not stale!"[27]

Lawrence had been dead for more than a decade when Bynner's

book about him was published. Yet the British author had immortalized Bynner and Johnson by casting them as the minor characters Owen Rhys and Bud Villiers in his 1926 novel *The Plumed Serpent*, Lawrence's fictionalized version of their trip to Mexico. During the book's opening scene at a bullfight, Lawrence employs a metaphor for the character Rhys (based on Bynner) that also describes his subject as juvenile: "His nose had a sharp look, like a little boy, who may make himself sick, but who is watching at the shambles with all his eyes, knowing it is forbidden."[28]

Kraft summarized the relationship thusly:

> If Lawrence saw Bynner as too gregarious, as hiding a fear of intimacy in a light-hearted manner, Bynner saw Lawrence as a man equally afraid of intimacy, as hiding behind his severe criticism of Frieda and much of the world he met. The intensity of what Lawrence and Bynner felt was very great, too great to allow them to relax together. Each had been understood and challenged in a dimension that was deep and important.[29]

Sharing a Life

While Bynner did not hide his homosexuality from Lawrence and other friends, he never openly addressed it in his work until the publication of *Eden Tree* in 1931, the year he turned fifty. While writing this poem, he began a relationship with twenty-four-year-old Robert Hunt that would last until Hunt's death in 1964. Hunt, the son of acclaimed California architect Myron Hunt, met Bynner in 1924, introduced by Paul Horgan, a novelist and historian who wrote Pulitzer Prize–winning books about New Mexico. They met again several times over the years, and when Hunt visited Santa Fe to recover from an illness in 1930, he and Bynner started their lifelong relationship. The two lived together openly, establishing a companionship that "was a marriage, in the sense that we mean a sharing together in life," Bynner's biographer wrote.[30]

Hunt's own interests paralleled Bynner's. He wrote poetry and designed some of the additions to Bynner's house as well as the renovation of a house he and Bynner bought on Atalaya Hill in Santa Fe. In 1940, the pair purchased a house in Chapala, Mexico, a part of the country that Bynner had first visited with the Lawrences and Spud Johnson.

Bynner and Hunt oversaw renovations to the house and enjoyed spending time in it, though not always together. Their relationship suffered when Hunt began drinking excessively, but they remained together. Hunt left to serve several stints in the U.S. Army during World War II, but his poor health kept him far from the battlefront, working on the docks and in an office instead. Bynner continued to write, publishing several more volumes of poetry including the 1955 *Book of Lyrics*, which Kraft called "a confident book, as if Bynner had decided not to compete anymore with the poetic world that had passed him by."[31] His final book, *New Poems 1960*, received glowing praise. He wrote it just after waking early in the mornings, composing poems that "read like inquiries into the mysteries and absurdities of our long, strange lives."[32] Poet William Carlos Williams described the book as "an unqualified piece of work that will be hard to equal for many a day."[33]

Bynner's life changed drastically when Hunt died suddenly of a heart attack in 1964. He had Hunt's ashes buried in the garden of their house on Atalaya Hill. Almost exactly one year later, Bynner suffered a stroke and never fully recovered. He lingered in a helpless state until he died on June 1, 1968; his ashes were placed next to Hunt's. He left the Atalaya Hill house and his adobe estate on Buena Vista Street to St. John's College, which turned the former into a home for the college president and the latter into a dormitory for students and teachers. Today, Bynner's beloved Buena Vista estate houses the Inn of the Turquoise Bear, whose owners have made Bynner a passion of their own, collecting stories they amiably share with guests about the famous poet who once lived and worked in the multistoried adobe. Bynner would appreciate that one of the inn's owners is named Robert Frost, though he bears no relation to the famous poet who once had his head doused with dregs from Bynner's ale.

Bynner wrote more than twenty-five published books of poetry and plays as well as translations that largely have been forgotten. The Witter Bynner Foundation for Poetry in Santa Fe, established by an endowment left by Bynner, supports poets and fosters an awareness of poetry with programs it funds around the country. The foundation also arranged the publication of a five-volume series of Bynner's writing, hoping to keep poets and poetry fans aware of his work.

Bynner's 1929 collection of poetry, *Indian Earth*, may be his best book. "The poems are written in a language and style that could be described as classic American," Kraft wrote.[34] *Indian Earth* contains lyrical poems about Chapala and about the Native Americans of the Southwest. In the following excerpt from one of those poems, "A Dance for Rain," Bynner offers his response to watching a ceremonial rain dance at Cochiti Pueblo:

> You may never see rain, unless you see
> A dance for rain at Cochiti,
> Never hear thunder in the air
> Unless you hear the thunder there,
> Nor know the lightning in the sky
> If there's no pole to know it by.
> They dipped the pole just as I came,
> And I can never be the same
> Since those feathers gave my brow
> The touch of wind that's on it now,
> Bringing over the arid lands
> Butterfly gestures from Hopi hands
> And holding me, till earth shall fail,
> As close to earth as a fox's tail.[35]

CHAPTER FOUR

Mary Austin

LIKE WITTER BYNNER, Mary Hunter Austin had already secured a high-profile literary reputation before moving to Santa Fe in 1924 and settling on Camino del Monte Sol. She chose to build her residence, an elegant adobe called Casa Querida (Spanish for "Beloved Home"), near the homes of both Bynner and Alice Corbin Henderson. Living in the heart of Santa Fe brought her in close contact with the Native American and Hispano cultures that nurtured her desire for a spiritual experience.

By then, Santa Fe and Taos had become known as literary colonies, thanks largely to the presence of Alice Corbin Henderson in Santa Fe and Mabel Dodge Luhan in Taos. Austin's arrival, however, did much to heighten the reputation of northern New Mexico's writers' colonies, as her prominent voice addressed many political and social topics of the day through her books, articles, and lectures. She wrote more than thirty books and upward of 250 articles, all filled with her distinctive voice and radical beliefs about women's rights, marriage, environmental issues, and the need for American art and literature to acknowledge and incorporate their indigenous roots. Her ideas were well ahead of her time, which sometimes made her work inaccessible to many readers. "Her convictions, always passionately felt and sometimes fractiously expressed, endeared her to some while often jeopardizing her career," her biographer Esther Lanigan Stineman pointed out.[1]

Olive Rush, "Portrait of Mary Austin," no date, oil on panel.
Collection of the Museum of Fine Arts, New Mexico.
Gift of the School of American Research, 1976.

Early Years

Austin was born Mary Hunter in 1868 in Carlinville, Illinois, and enjoyed a close relationship with her father, an esteemed Civil War hero who introduced her to classic writers including Herman Melville, Ralph Waldo Emerson, John Keats, and Elizabeth Barrett Browning. She was one of four children, but at the age of ten she lost her father and younger sister to illness, which left her with a difficult and distant mother. During these lonely years, she sought comfort nurturing a mystical connection with nature.

Austin's 1931 book *Experiences Facing Death* describes a powerful epiphany she experienced as a young girl relating to the natural world, which forever altered her experience of life. One summer morning, walking alone through an orchard near her home, she stood on a grass-covered hill beneath a walnut tree and became abruptly and profoundly aware of the connections between all living things—"I in them and they in me, and all of us enclosed in a warm lucent bubble of living-ness"—and from this moment on, she felt in touch with a powerful source that gave birth to all of life.[2]

The experience later informed much of Austin's writing about the environment, including her famous 1903 masterpiece *The Land of Little Rain*. This book of essays, first serialized in *Atlantic Monthly* magazine, explored how humans could live with nature rather than battle to control it, based on examples drawn from Native American culture.

Austin encountered indigenous Americans upon moving to California with her family in 1888, following her graduation from Blackburn College in Carlinville, where she studied science. The family chose the southern San Joaquin Valley because Austin's older brother had homesteaded there, and they arrived during the first year of a bad three-year drought. The lack of rain caused serious devastation, yet Austin enjoyed exploring the arid country, familiarizing herself with the plant and animal life as well as the people who worked the land.

Austin found work as a schoolteacher and, in 1891, married rancher Wallace Austin, who also taught school. The couple moved the following year to Owens Valley, where Austin's husband planned to irrigate and then plant vineyards with his brother. While he worked, she began to write poems, stories, and articles and learn about the culture from neighboring Native Americans and Hispanos. In this part of the country, she began to get in touch with what she later called the

American Rhythm, the title of her 1923 book that urged a return to the rhythms and poetry of the Native Americans. Austin believed that America's indigenous people carried the true American rhythm, which emerged from an intense relationship to the land and the seasons and cycles of nature. She developed her theory to counter the widespread opinion that America's rhythm was rooted in the classic poetry and music of Europe.

In 1892, Austin gave birth to a daughter, Ruth, who was developmentally disabled. That same year, Austin saw her first work published when *Overland Monthly* magazine accepted her short story "The Mother of Felipe." What conflicting emotions Austin must have felt. During her pregnancy, she had every reason to believe she would give birth to a highly intelligent child. Only after the birth did she discover that her husband had kept his family's "tainted inheritance" from her, in keeping with the custom of the times to never talk about such problems.[3] While Austin then blamed her husband for their daughter's condition, her own Methodist mother considered the tragedy to be a "judgment" upon her daughter for rejecting a conventional lifestyle suited to the women of that time.[4] Austin's marriage, already suffering because her husband's financial endeavors kept failing, began a downward spiral that would end in divorce in 1914. The demands of being Ruth's primary caregiver took their toll, causing Austin to suffer a nervous breakdown in 1898. Later that year, she escaped her unhappy home life by checking herself into a San Francisco hospital. There she met the great American psychologist and philosopher William James, and their conversations about creativity and the unconscious would greatly influence Austin's work.

According to Stineman, "Mary reiterated throughout her life that Ruth's illness was an expensive burden, and the Austins most certainly lacked the means to place her in a private sanatorium before the success of Mary's first book."[5] The situation changed with the publication of *The Land of Little Rain*, which Austin wrote after meeting Charles Lummis in Los Angeles in 1899 and joining his circle of influential writers. Her mentorship with Lummis, a well-known journalist, photographer, and author of the acclaimed *The Land of Poco Tiempo*, helped open publishing doors to Austin, who launched her reputation as an intuitive and sensitive nature writer with *The Land of Little Rain*. The book contained fourteen essays that captured life in California's arid desert, arguing for the need to give back power over their land to Native Americans. "The transformation of the observation into precisely crafted and compelling prose constitutes the triumph of the text," Stineman wrote.[6]

Austin's next book, *The Basket Woman*, appeared in 1904, containing a collection of children's stories drawn from Paiute and Shoshone myths. In 1905, she published her first novel, *Isidro*, followed by *The Flock*, a history of sheep and sheepherding in California. The money she earned from these books allowed her to make the difficult decision in 1904 to place her daughter in an institution in Santa Clara, despite her husband's protestations. The following year she committed Ruth permanently. Her daughter remained in the institution until she died from pneumonia in 1918.

Austin then immersed herself in her literary career, settling in Carmel, California, where she helped create a colony of writers and artists that included writers Jack London, Ambrose Bierce, and George Sterling. Her literary success enabled her to buy land and build a house in Carmel. In 1907, her husband charged her with desertion but their marriage did not officially end in divorce until 1914.

After discovering she had breast cancer in 1907, Austin decided to see the world, embarking on a trip to Europe that lasted for two years. In part, the journey was a search for a spiritual remedy, and it worked. She returned to the United States in 1910, settled in New York City, and wrote six more books. Her 1912 novel *Woman of Genius* became her most praised work of fiction, perhaps because it parallels her own struggle of becoming a successful woman writer. The novel follows one woman's attempts to become a serious actress. While in New York Austin also became a playwright, though with less success. When her play about a Native American medicine woman, *The Arrow-Maker*, opened in 1911 on Broadway, it ran for only three weeks and was not well received. Also in New York, Austin attended some of the fashionable salons hosted by Luhan, which brought together the movers and shakers of the moment. Luhan's biographer Lois Palken Rudnick has theorized that at one of these salons, Austin may have given a lecture that first introduced Luhan to Native American cultures.[7]

After the United States became involved in World War I and her friend Herbert Hoover became the head of the National Food

Administration, Austin took on a new job. Under Hoover's leadership, she joined the administration's propaganda corps in 1917 and traveled the country to help establish community kitchens and victory gardens.

Drawn to Santa Fe

As the war drew to an end, Austin's thoughts turned to where she might settle next. She returned to Carmel, only to find that it had become a tourist town. In 1918, she took a trip to New Mexico and, like so many other authors, activists, and artists of the time, stayed with Luhan in Taos. Visiting Santa Fe that same year, she helped establish the Community

Mary Austin, date unknown.
Courtesy Palace of the Governors (MNM/DCA). Neg. no. 45221.

Theatre, organizing a debut production featuring Spanish and English plays and songs as well as stage sets that she persuaded Santa Fe artists Gustave Baumann and Carlos Vierra to design. (The group officially incorporated in 1919 as the Santa Fe Little Theatre, which remains active today as the Santa Fe Playhouse.) After that visit, Austin declared she would one day make her home in northern New Mexico.

In 1923, Austin returned for a driving tour of the Southwest with painter Gerald Cassidy and his wife, Ina Sizer Cassidy, who mined New Mexican culture and traditions for her poetry, short stories, and magazine articles. The intent of this trip was to collect information for *The Land of Journey's Ending*, a companion book to *The Land of Little Rain*. In his book *Southwest Classics*, Lawrence Clark Powell described *The Land of Journey's Ending*, published in 1924, as the book "that best embodies the essences of the region whose heartland is Arizona and Mexico."[8]

In 1924, Austin decided to make Santa Fe her permanent home, citing three reasons: "It is a mountain country, immensely dramatically beautiful: it is contiguous to the desert with its appeal of mystery and naked space; and it supplies the element of aboriginal society which I have learned to recognize as my proper medium."[9]

A fourth factor for choosing Santa Fe over Taos might well have been Luhan, whose domineering presence in Taos kept Austin at a safe distance. To Austin, Luhan "never gained credibility as an artist or serious writer" and "while Austin freely availed herself of Luhan's hospitality, these two formidable women frequently disagreed on a variety of topics."[10]

Austin's intuition about Santa Fe proved correct, as she wrote in *Earth Horizon*: "Once having determined upon Santa Fe as my future home, I never quite let go of it."[11] She became a major member of the Santa Fe literary community to the extent that both friends and foes referred to her as God's-Mother-in-Law. Even before she had settled there permanently, she became involved in the fight against the Bursum Bill, adding her voice to the outcry from other local as well as national writers opposed to the U.S. government's attempts to take away land rights from the Native American pueblos. (See chapter 7 for more information about the Bursum Bill.)

Activism had appealed to Austin well before she moved to Santa Fe. In the Owens Valley, she fought for water rights, which helped to lay the groundwork for the battle she joined in 1927 as a delegate to the Boulder Dam Conference, where she tried to block plans to divert water from the Colorado River to Los Angeles. She became a staunch supporter, too, of women's rights, arguing especially for the right to vote and to use birth control.

An avid collector of Southwest art, Austin helped establish the Indian Arts Fund in 1925, a permanent collection of art by Pueblo people as well as other Southwest tribes. She also helped arrange the restoration of the historic Santuario de Chimayó in Chimayó, New Mexico, and was one of the founders of the Spanish Colonial Arts Society, which continues to be devoted to the preservation and promotion of Spanish Colonial art traditions.

When Austin decided to build her abode home on Camino del Monte Sol, she hired her friend and neighbor Frank Applegate, an artist and architect, to oversee the construction. During his time in the Southwest, Applegate had become a serious collector of Native American and Spanish Colonial art. He encouraged a number of artists in the Santa Fe art colony to make their own adobe bricks and build houses and studios near his adobe on Camino del Monte Sol.

In "Frank Applegate," an article Austin wrote for the *New Mexico Quarterly Review*, she revealed that she convinced Applegate to write down amusing stories he had encountered while collecting the Native American art he treasured. He took her advice, penning tales that were published in his 1929 book *Indian Stories from the Pueblos*. Applegate had begun a second book filled with regional tales from Native American, Spanish, and Anglo cultures when he died suddenly in 1931, before he could complete the project. In her article, Austin wrote that she completed the book, which was published in 1932 as *Native Tales of New Mexico*.[12]

Austin's seven-room adobe "was spacious and seemed more so because of its sparse furnishings. With its sitting room and small library for reading and an office to write in, it was a home built for work."[13] The residence became a center for literary and artistic events. After the launching of the Poets' Roundup reading series, for instance, Austin hosted one of the annual events in the garden of Casa Querida. The Arsuna School of Fine Arts also took up residence in her house while Austin lived there, which is fitting since an art gallery now occupies Austin's house.

End of a Starry Adventure

Austin's final novel, *Starry Adventure*, was published in 1931, three years before her death in 1934 from a heart attack at age sixty-five. Its hopeful story concerns a young Anglo boy who arrives in New Mexico with his family so that his father can recover from tuberculosis. Even though his father dies and the family suffers financial difficulty, the protagonist grows up, marries, and gleans that beneath New Mexico's wide, open skies, his life has been full of "starry adventure." Austin's biographer claimed that this book contained a synthesis of the major themes that Austin wrote about throughout her life: "the timeless beauty of the 'the landscape line'; the essential nobility of indigenous inhabitants of the land, contrasted with the shallowness and corruption of eastern literati; and the superiority of the essential woman over the so-called New Woman.[14] To some extent, *Starry Adventure* paralleled Austin's own life, from the loss of her father and her failures with marriage and motherhood to her discovery of "the beauty, the mystery, and charm of New Mexico."[15]

Despite the serious themes of her work, Austin was not above satirizing the social life of the writers in northern New Mexico. Even though she and Luhan established a friendship, she parodied the famous Taos arts patron in *Starry Adventure* through the character Eudora Ballantine, a wealthy arts patron living in a grand home in Taos. As Luhan's biographer Lois Palken Rudnick pointed out, Ballantine mirrors Luhan. Ballantine collects people, seducing the novel's hero and finally marrying a Hispano aristocrat "merely for the cachet of adding him to her collection of indigenous items."[16] Rudnick described Ballantine's husband as "the final ornament in the restoration of her villa," which she intends to be a "playground" for her "fashionable Eastern friends."[17] As a later chapter on Luhan reveals, Luhan attempted to turn her Taos estate into a similar kind of center.

When *Earth Horizon*, Austin's memoir, was published in 1932 two years before her death, it outsold her other books, landing a spot on the Literary Guild's recommended reading list. The autobiography revealed, through a creative transition between first- and third-person narrators, how Austin's childhood contributed to shaping her life-long commitment to women's rights and Indian rights, as well as her passion for promoting the preservation of literature and art of the American Indian and Hispano cultures. The book's title came from the

Zia Pueblo symbol for earth horizon, which Austin described as "the incalculable blue ring of sky meeting earth," and a symbol for what she had spent her life pursuing—"the nurture of the spiritual life."[18] In the wide, open spaces of the Southwest, Austin finally found a home that deeply nourished her need for spiritual inspiration. As she explained in *The Land of Little Rain*,

> For all the toll the desert takes of a man it gives compensations, deep breaths, deep sleep, and the communion of the stars . . . It is hard to escape the sense of mastery as the stars move in the wide clear heavens to risings and settings unobscured. They look large and near and palpitant; as if they moved on some stately surface not needful to declare. Wheeling to their stations in the sky, they make the poor world-fret of no account. Of no account you who lie out there watching, nor the lean coyote that stands off in the scrub from you and howls and howls.[19]

CHAPTER FIVE

Willa Cather

WILLA CATHER, one of the most venerated authors connected to the New Mexico literary colonies, did not feel the same pull to settle in the Southwest that had drawn Witter Bynner, Alice Corbin Henderson, Mary Austin, and others. But New Mexico's history intrigued her, especially where it intersected with French history, for Cather greatly admired the art and culture of France. Thus it seemed inevitable that she would write a fictionalized account of the life of Archbishop Jean Baptiste Lamy, a Frenchman who became New Mexico's first archbishop. *Death Comes for the Archbishop* deftly explores how the untamed country of New Mexico changes a man of the church, even as he struggles to impose his faith upon that country's people. Since its publication in 1927, the novel has remained a best-selling classic in the region.

Many critics and scholars consider Cather to be the first great female American novelist. She won the Pulitzer Prize in 1923 for her novel *One of Ours*, and already was firmly established in the country's literary realm when, during one of her several visits to Santa Fe, she discovered the story of Lamy, which compelled her to write *Death Comes for the Archbishop*.

Willa Cather, date unknown. Photo by Nickolas Muray.
Courtesy Palace of the Governors (MNM/DCA). Neg. no. 111734.

A Momentous Uprooting

Cather was born in 1873 in Black Creek, Virginia, as the first of seven children. Her family's success at farming made them prominent citizens. When she was nine, she and her family moved to Nebraska so her father could farm, following in the footsteps of his father. But hardships ensued, forcing the family to uproot themselves once again, this time from the Nebraska country to the nearby railroad town of Red Cloud, Nebraska, where her father took a job in a real estate and loan office.

Leaving Virginia, a lush land filled with trees, mountains, and a conservative class of people, for the stark, flat landscape of Nebraska, populated mostly by European immigrants, greatly affected Cather. Her friend, novelist Dorothy Canfield, later said that the move from Virginia to Nebraska became central to Cather's fiction, as Cather experienced powerful emotions about exchanging one landscape for another at an impressionable age.[1] As Cather herself wrote in a short autobiography for her publisher, Alfred Knopf, Virginia was an "old conservative society" where "life was ordered and settled, where the people in good families were born good, and the poor mountain people were not expected to amount to much."[2] Nebraska's equivalent of the struggling mountain people, the European immigrants, held vast appeal for the young Cather. "No child with a spark of generosity could have kept from throwing herself heart and soul into the fight these people were making to master the language, to master the soil, to hold their land and to get ahead in the world," Cather wrote in her autobiography for Knopf.[3] She would feel a similarly powerful pull in her heart upon discovering the Southwest.

As she moved from adolescence to young adulthood, Cather was painfully aware of the limitations of her gender. The customs of Victorian society dictated that she become a wife and mother rather than pursue any type of serious career. Instead of accepting that role, she fought against society's expectations, dressing as a boy and renaming herself William Cather Jr. She even enrolled at the University of Nebraska as William, intent on studying medicine and becoming a surgeon. But once she began to express herself with words on paper, the path of her life became clear. She was a still a college student when nine of her short stories were published, primarily in college journals, and she wrote more than three hundred reviews and articles, including some as the drama critic for the *Nebraska State Journal*.

A Writer's Life Unfolds

Upon graduating from college, Cather went to Pittsburgh to become the editor of a new family magazine, *Home Monthly*. When the magazine was sold in 1897, nearly a year after Cather had started the job, she began writing drama and literary reviews for the *Pittsburgh Leader* newspaper. She soon grew bored with the details of journalism work, however, and resigned from the newspaper in 1900 to teach high school English and Latin at Pittsburgh's Central High School for a few years, hoping to focus on her writing.

In Pittsburgh in 1899, Cather began an important relationship that would greatly impact her life when, in the dressing room of an actress, she met Isabel McClung, a wealthy young woman from Pittsburgh. They established a close friendship that many scholars have interpreted as romantic. (Cather avoided writing about lesbian or gay themes because she knew that they generally were not accepted at the time.) McClung's family invited Cather to move into their upscale Pittsburgh home and transformed their attic sewing room into a writing study for her. In this space, Cather wrote *April Twilights*, her first book and only collection of poetry, published in 1903. (She financed the book's publication herself.) She also wrote *The Troll Garden*, her debut collection of stories, in the McClungs' attic study. Cather sent *The Troll Garden* in manuscript form to S. S. McClure, publisher of *McClure's Magazine* and head of McClure Phillips, a New York publishing company. McClure agreed to print two of her short stories from *The Troll Garden* in his magazine and also to publish *The Troll Garden* as a book in 1905. McClure was so impressed by her writing that he traveled to Pittsburgh to offer Cather a job at his magazine. She accepted, and within two years became managing editor of the influential literary and political magazine.

Her friendship with Isabel McClung remained important to her personal life as well as her work. McClung served as a muse to Cather and read her work with an editor's eye. In the summer of 1902, they journeyed together to England and France to visit sites connected to artists Cather admired. They grew so close that when Isabel McClung decided to marry a violinist in 1916, the decision devastated Cather. Overwhelmed by the loss, she may have chosen to write her way through it later, transforming her sorrow into creativity by producing novels about two memorable women—*My Antonia*, published in 1918, and *A Lost Lady*, published in 1923.

Despite her affection for McClung, Cather was able to develop a bond with another woman who became her companion for the rest of her life. She first met Edith Lewis in 1903 at an editor's house in Lincoln, Nebraska. A recent graduate of Smith College, Lewis already was a fan of Cather's work, having read some of her newspaper articles as well as *April Twilights*. In 1908, Lewis became Cather's work editor. Eventually, the two women moved to New York City, where they lived together until Cather's death in 1947.

Not until Cather met acclaimed New England writer Sarah Orne Jewett, author of *The Country of the Pointed Firs*, did she begin to reconsider her chosen career as a journalist. Jewett, who became a mentor to Cather, made it clear in a 1909 letter she wrote to Cather that she believed serious writers should never work as journalists: "Your vivid, exciting companionship in the office must not be your audience, you must find your own quiet centre of life, and write from that to the world that holds offices, and all society, all Bohemia; the city, the country—in short, you must write to the human heart."[4]

In the Southwest

Cather acted on Jewett's advice, taking a leave of absence in 1912 from *McClure's Magazine* so that she could work on her debut novel, *Alexander's Bridge*, published that same year. Also in 1912, Cather took her first trip to the Southwest. She journeyed to Winslow, Arizona, to visit her brother, who worked for the Atchison, Topeka, and Santa Fe Railway, and she stopped in Albuquerque too. The trip was meant to help Cather recover from a minor illness. During the two months she spent in Winslow, she and her brother rode horses, visited cliff dwellings, and attended the Hopi Snake Dance. The trip not only restored her health, it lifted her spirits immensely. She wrote to McClure that she had not felt so happy since she was a child.

Cather was so impressed with Albuquerque that she sent a letter to a friend, journalist Elizabeth Shepley Sergeant, encouraging Sergeant to visit the city. In her biography, *Willa Cather: A Memoir*, Sergeant explained why the Albuquerque region so entranced Cather: "In this Rio Grande region the grandiose and historical scale of things seemed to forecast some great spiritual event—something certainly that had nothing to do with the appalling mediocrity and vulgarity of the industrial civilization."[5]

This 1912 trip impacted Cather's work. As Sergeant wrote in *Willa Cather: A Memoir*, the Southwest utterly changed Cather: "The vast solitude of the Southwest, its bald, magnificence, brilliant light and physical impact, too, had the effect of toning up her spirit, and made available a path in which a new artistic method could evolve from familiar Nebraska subject matter."[6]

After the Southwest trip, Cather wrote with a strong sense of place, illuminating the intimate ties between the vast prairies of Nebraska and the people who lived on and worked the land. She returned to Nebraska and then to stay with her friend Isabel McClung in Pittsburgh, where she immediately began work on her classic book about Nebraska, *O Pioneers!* Published in 1913, the novel is considered by many to be her best and it earned her a reputation as a writer of stature. In one short passage from *O Pioneers!* Cather eloquently summed up her belief about the power of place: "We come and go, but the land is always here," says Alexander Bergson, the novel's fiercely independent Swedish heroine. "And the people who love it and understand it are the people who own it—for a little while."[7]

Cather wove her feelings about the Southwest into her 1915 novel *The Song of the Lark*, which focused on a young opera singer, Thea Kronborg, a character inspired by real-life opera singer Olive Fremstad, whom Cather had interviewed for a *McClure's* article. Kronborg's epiphany, which takes place when she first views Arizona's San Francisco Mountains, presumably parallels what Cather felt upon first witnessing the landscape of the Southwest:

> The personality of which she was so tired seemed to let go of her. The high, sparkling air drank it up like blotting-paper. It was lost in the thrilling blue of the new sky and the song of the thin wind in the *piñons*. The old, fretted lines which marked one off, which defined her—made her Thea Kronborg, Bower's accompanist, a soprano with a faulty middle voice—were all erased.[8]

Encountering the Archbishop

The Southwest had cast its spell on Cather. She returned with Edith Lewis in the summer of 1915 to explore Mesa Verde in Colorado and Taos. In 1916, she made yet another visit, this time to Santa Fe,

Espanola, and Santa Cruz, but the writers' colonies in Santa Fe and Taos had not yet formed. It wasn't until Cather returned with Lewis in the summer of 1925 that she would find Mary Austin in Santa Fe and Mabel Dodge Luhan in Taos. On this trip she also discovered a copy of W. J. Howlett's *The Life of the Right Reverend Joseph P. Machebeuf—Pioneer Priest of New Mexico*, which sparked the idea for Cather's classic novel *Death Comes for the Archbishop*.

Cather read Howlett's book in a solitary night while staying at La Fonda, a fashionable Santa Fe hotel. It concerned the life of Machebeuf, a Roman Catholic priest who had accompanied Jean Baptiste Lamy from France to Ohio in 1839 and then on to New Mexico in 1851. As soon as she finished reading the book, she saw the plot of her novel. It would focus on Bishop Latour, based on the real-life character of Lamy, and his friend and associate Father Vaillant, based on Joseph Machebeuf. Her novel also would reflect her feelings about the potency of the Southwest:

> As the wagons went forward and the sun sank lower, a sweep of red carnelian-coloured hills lying at the foot of the mountains came into view; they curved like two arms about a depression in the plain; and in that depression was Santa Fé, at last! A thin wavering adobe town . . . a green plaza . . . at one end, a church with two earthen towers that rose high above the flatness. The long main street began at the church, the town seemed to flow from it like a stream from a spring.[9]

During that 1925 trip to Santa Fe, Luhan invited Cather to spend some time in Taos, and Cather was delighted to meet Luhan's husband, Tony Luhan. According to Luhan's biographer, Lois Palken Rudnick, Luhan suggested Cather and Lewis spend a few days in the Pink House, one of the guesthouses on her estate. Cather so enjoyed riding around in Tony Luhan's car, listening to him sing Pueblo songs and tell engaging stories about New Mexico's land and people, that she decided to stay for two weeks instead.[10] In her biography, *Willa Cather Living*, Edith Lewis wrote that she believed Tony Luhan had such an impact on Cather, she decided to use him as the model for the Navajo character Eusabio in *Death Comes for the Archbishop*.[11]

For Cather, the most important story to be told about the early

Southwest was how the missionary priests struggled to establish the Roman Catholic Church in an untamed country. This belief brought disapproval from Santa Fe author Mary Austin. Once *Death Comes for the Archbishop* was published, Austin was "distressed" that Cather had chosen to write about an aspect of New Mexico history from the sympathetic perspective of a French missionary, effectively eclipsing the prevalent Hispano history that took root in the region much earlier.[12]

When *Death Comes for the Archbishop* was published in 1927, Cather inscribed a copy to Austin: "For Mary Austin, in whose lovely study I wrote the last chapters of this book. She will be my sternest critic—and she has the right to be. I will always take a calling-down from my betters."[13] Yet scholars have debated whether Cather actually did write any part of the novel in Austin's home. The details are confusing. Cather returned to Santa Fe in June 1926 for one final visit before completing her manuscript in the fall of 1926. She rented a hotel room at La Fonda. Austin, who was then a patient at a hospital in St. Louis, Missouri, had invited Cather to make use of her home while she was gone. After the novel was published, Austin claimed that Cather had sat in a chair in her library to write the book. Cather's journalist friend Sergeant insisted Austin was wrong. Cather had told her, Sergeant wrote, that she "sometimes walked up to Mrs. Austin's in the afternoon to write a few letters" and that she "had left her manuscript in a vault in New York City.[14] But T. M. Pearce, who assembled and edited Mary Austin's letters for the *Literary America* series, surmised from her inscription that Cather indeed might have worked on the book that afternoon in Austin's study.[15] Perhaps Austin's admonishment upset Cather enough to deny having worked on it in her home. Or, maybe Austin's desire for the kind of fame Cather achieved led her to forge the inscription and make up a story connecting her to the novel. At any rate, Cather never returned to Santa Fe.

After her final visit to New Mexico in 1926, Cather continued to write novels, short stories, and a book of essays. She earned numerous awards, including the 1944 Gold Medal of the National Institute of Arts and Letters. She died in New York on April 24, 1947, at age 74, and was buried not in New Mexico, but on a hill in Jaffrey, New Hampshire, a place she had often retreated to while writing.

Unlike other writers who had fallen under New Mexico's spell, Cather never had the urge to settle in the Southwest. Perhaps the social scenes in Taos and Santa Fe were simply too much for a writer who had heeded Sarah Orne Jewett's advice to locate her own "quiet centre of life" and, from there, write to "the human heart." In that center, Cather found an immense understanding of how a land can shape its people, and then produced some of the most acclaimed literature of the twentieth century.

CHAPTER SIX

Oliver La Farge

OLIVER LA FARGE, best known for his coming-of-age novel *Laughing Boy*, did not settle permanently in Santa Fe until 1941, after the writers' colonies had reached their peak. He spent so much time in Santa Fe and the Southwest, however, that much of his work reflects the same passion for Native American life that imbued the work of many of the writers of the literary golden era in Santa Fe and Taos.

Laughing Boy, a Navajo love story set in 1915, won the Pulitzer Prize in 1930 and earned its author the unwelcome distinction of being a writer who focused solely on Native Americans. Yet he also produced an impressive body of short stories, essays, biography, memoir, social commentary, and ethnographical studies. His diverse subject matter included modern life in Santa Fe, ranch life in northern New Mexico, an artist's life in New Orleans, and studies of the Mayan culture.

The son of a distinguished family from Saunderstown, Rhode Island, La Farge graduated cum laude from Harvard, where he earned a fellowship to do graduate studies in anthropology. He completed his master's degree in 1929, the same year that *Laughing Boy* was published, and then spent years dividing his time between his interests as an ethnologist and as a writer. He established a solid literary career. "As a professional man of letters in his adopted region, La Farge's position in Southwestern writing is a secure one."[1] Yet he never left behind his

Oliver La Farge, date unknown.
Courtesy Palace of the Governors (MNM/DCA). Neg. no. 16741.

academic training, as "the scientist in La Farge demanded that portrayals of culture and character be true to his data," wrote David L. Caffey in his introduction to *Yellow Sun, Bright Sky*, a collection of La Farge's short stories about Native Americans. "Though he knew his stories had to be entertaining above all else if they were to sell, La Farge was not unaware of the potential for influencing attitudes toward Indians through his writing."[2]

Indian Man

Born in 1901 in New York City, La Farge's early years at his family's summer home in Saunderstown, Rhode Island, brought him in touch with the stories and history of Native American tribes of the East Coast. With dark straight hair and high cheekbones, La Farge himself bore enough of a resemblance to Native Americans that his mother nicknamed him Indian Man, according to La Farge's biographer D'Arcy McNickle.[3]

As an undergraduate at Harvard, La Farge lived up to that nickname, making his first anthropological foray into Native American country of the Southwest during the summer of 1921 when he joined a field party exploring the Four Corners area to establish a timeline of prehistory in the Southwest. He returned the following summer and again in the summer of 1924 after graduating from Harvard—this time overseeing his own crew of workers. La Farge concluded after these summers that he was not drawn to anthropology, but rather "the living, singing, free-moving Navajo Indians were suddenly a new force in his life. To live among them and to become knowledgeable about their ways of life seemed to answer his need for a focal point around which to organize his energies."[4] That force grew even stronger when the 1924 field work ended and La Farge, joined by two companions, journeyed through Navajo country and Hopi land on horseback, befriending the native people and honing the basics of Navajo language.

From these field trips, La Farge gathered material for his Harvard master's degree thesis on the "Derivation of Apache and Navajo Culture." "Indians became the dominant theme of his life," Caffey wrote. "They engaged his intellect as a scientist, his imagination as a writer, and his passion as a man of social responsibility. Indian religion provided the key to his own spiritual liberation, Indian issues the substance of his political agenda."[5]

Laughing Boy

La Farge's experiences in the Southwest earned him a position as an ethnology assistant in 1926 at Tulane University's Department of Middle American Research during his graduate studies at Harvard. When he wasn't a member of several Tulane expeditions exploring the Indian cultures of southern Mexico and Guatemala, he lived in the French Quarter of New Orleans, where he joined a group of budding writers that included William Faulkner. There, undoubtedly inspired by his literary companions as well as his time among the Navajo, he wrote *Laughing Boy*, snatching moments to work on the book when he wasn't writing reports about the Tulane expeditions toward his master's degree, which he earned from Harvard University in 1929.

La Farge's biographer reported that *Laughing Boy* did not flow easily from its author. The novel took so much time to create that La Farge began to write articles and short stories, submitting them to magazines with the hopes of earning some income. In 1927, *The Dial*, a small literary magazine, accepted "North Is Black," his short story about a Navajo man. The story caught the attention of an editor at Houghton Mifflin who wondered whether La Farge might be working on a novel about the Navajo drawn from his own experiences in the Southwest. When La Farge sent along his outline and incomplete manuscript, Houghton Mifflin's positive interest provided the impetus he needed to complete *Laughing Boy*. As La Farge had just lost his job at Tulane and was seriously questioning whether he could become a professional writer, things could not have worked out better. Published in 1929, *Laughing Boy* quickly became a success. "A number of reviewers commented on how skillfully La Farge had caught the simple, direct language of the Indian characters; one reviewer went so far as to say that the author had managed to think like an Indian."[6]

More success followed. *Laughing Boy* became a book club edition of the Literary Guild and was published in England before winning the Pulitzer Prize in May 1930. It helped that Mary Austin sat on the panel of Pulitzer judges for she was keenly aware that the East Coast literary establishment would have difficulty accepting a story about Native Americans as serious literature. Austin declared that out of all the books she'd come across, *Laughing Boy* offered "the nearest approach to a genuine primitive love story."[7] Others agreed, for publishers in France, Germany, Poland, Holland, Sweden, and Norway bought the foreign publishing rights and Universal Pictures acquired the film rights in 1931, even paying for La Farge to travel to Hollywood and audition, unsuccessfully, for the lead role. (Problems arose at Universal with the story's subject matter, so MGM finally released the film in 1934. It starred Ramon Navarro and Lupe Velez, though it failed to become a hit. *Laughing Boy* also became a stage play that did not achieve success.)

Once *Laughing Boy* had been accepted for publication, La Farge left New Orleans and married Wanden Matthews, a New York debutante, in the fall of 1929. He continued his interests in ethnology as a research associate at the University of Pennsylvania from 1929 to 1931, when he worked on manuscripts from the university's collection related to the Mayan culture. Eventually he published two papers that reexamined the history of the Mayan people through the evolution of their language. Both papers "have remained landmarks in the development of Mayan studies."[8]

Working in Two Worlds

Befitting a man who had spent so much time traveling, La Farge did not settle in one place, but moved around from a New York City apartment to his family's Rhode Island home, a cattle ranch owned by his wife's family in Colorado Springs, Colorado, and a rented home in Santa Fe. His work on behalf of Native Americans became more intense when the Eastern Association on Indian Affairs, one of several groups initially formed to fight the Bursum Bill of 1922, appointed La Farge to its board of directors in 1930. He became president of the association in 1932. The position allowed him "a means of making practical use of the knowledge about the Indian people he had gained through research and personal contact."[9]

That summer, La Farge immersed himself in Native American life during a pack trip to the Southwest with his wife. He visited the Jicarilla Reservation to report about the conditions of life there to the association. The Apaches he got to know on the Jicarilla Reservation taught him much about the tough living conditions they endured after being forced to leave their homes for confinement on the reservation in northwestern New Mexico. La Farge also established a close and abiding connection with Santa Clara Pueblo through two brothers he befriended there. All of these experiences drove him to pursue "an enlightened policy" for the Native Americans, one that attempted to keep their culture intact instead of forcing assimilation.[10]

After this trip to the Southwest, La Farge returned to New York hoping to continue writing, but he also had become deeply committed to Indian affairs. He worked hard at both jobs, writing two novels and numerous short stories and articles between 1930 and 1935 to help support his growing family, which included a son, born in 1931, and a daughter, born in 1933. Literary fame continued when his "Haunted Ground" won the O. Henry Award for best short story in 1931 and Brown University bestowed on him an honorary master's degree in 1932 for focusing on the "sometimes neglected racial groups in our national life."[11] La Farge's second novel, *Sparks Fly Upward*, focused on an Indian battling for Indian rights in Latin America and received critical praise when it was published in 1931.

With his third novel, La Farge veered away from the two subjects that had occupied his fiction—ethnology and Native Americans. Well aware of his reputation as a writer who specialized in Indian stories, La Farge wanted to try his hand at other subject matter. Thus *Long Pennant*—published in 1933—explores New England privateers during the war of 1812, set on the seas and in Rhode Island and New Orleans. The book's disappointing sales resulted from the Depression era rather than La Farge's writing skills, but its failure did not help his marriage, which had begun to suffer because his writing was not lucrative enough for his wife.

Before accepting a job in 1936 with the Bureau of Indian Affairs assisting the Hopi, La Farge began the first of only two more major novels he would write—*The Enemy Gods*, which once again drew from his knowledge of the Navajos. As with his previous novels, La Farge worked slowly, starting the book in late 1935 and completing it in June 1937. Published in the fall of 1937, *The Enemy Gods* exhibited La Farge's understanding that "while biological extinction might indeed be [the Native Americans'] fate, the quality of Indianness would remain until the last singing voice was silenced."[12] The story about a Navajo man raised in an Anglo world and taught the tenets of Christianity who then reconnects with his own culture reflected La Farge's own belief, particularly when the hero of *The Enemy Gods* states, "If we want to save ourselves, we have to learn to use the white man's knowledge, his weapons, his machines—and still be Navajos."[13]

La Farge worked arduously to help the Native Americans retain their culture in the face of an encroaching white man's world. From the 1930s on, his reputation as a Native American expert brought him into the political fray and greatly interrupted his life as a professional writer. His desire to help the Southwest tribes he had come to know so well landed him an important job when the U.S. government launched its first major attempt to help tribes establish self-government, thereby protecting their culture. This attempt marked an abrupt change from the government's earlier attempts at tribal assimilation.

John Collier, commissioner of Indian Affairs, was the architect of the government's new approach, known as the Indian Reorganization Act of 1934, or the New Deal for Indians. Collier had the support of President Franklin Roosevelt, who backed the plan. Like La Farge, Collier was vehemently opposed to assimilation so it made sense that he looked to La Farge to help establish a constitution with the Hopi people—a difficult task because the Hopi lived in ten separate villages rather than as an assembled tribe. This was just one of many assignments La Farge took on throughout his life, hoping that the Native Americans of the Southwest would survive with their culture intact.

From the moment he first encountered Native people, La Farge carried a deep respect for who they were. Searching for a way to describe his feeling, he once wrote, "When I look in my own memory for the essences of what I've so loved in Indian camps, the summation of it, I find a tricky rhythm tapped out on a drum, a clear voice singing, and the sound of laughter."[14]

La Farge's biographer believed that La Farge "wrote best when he dealt with Native American themes and characters."[15] Clearly, his novels and short stories brought the culture to life for cadres of readers who had never before encountered Native Americans, as well as for those who knew them well. Yet he did write about other subjects. The *New Yorker* began to run his short stories as early as 1938, including a series about life on a ranch in a northern New Mexico mountain town. La Farge also wrote a popular column that covered an array of topics for the daily newspaper *Santa Fe New Mexican*, from 1950 until his death in 1963.

A New Life in Santa Fe

La Farge's first marriage ended in divorce in 1937, and though the loss was difficult, it was not surprising. "A basic incompatibility had always existed," his biographer wrote, adding, "Although obscured in the first years by the enthusiasms of success, it came sharply into view when success receded and the drudgery of a writer's life remained. If he had been willing or constitutionally inclined to seek full-time employment, or if he had consented to pursue success as measured by literary sales, their marriage might have lasted longer."[16] La Farge described the divorce to his brother as "the end of years of struggling against a steady resistance."[17]

La Farge began a new, more fulfilling union with Consuelo Baca, the daughter of a prominent New Mexico family from the mountain village of Rociada, whom he married in 1939. The couple traveled together through Hopi country, spent time in New York, and then settled permanently in Santa Fe in 1941. By then, he had begun his last novel, *The Copper Pot*, published in 1942, which marked his second attempt at writing a non–Native American–themed novel. His biographer outlined the many parallels between La Farge's early life and this novel about a New England painter who attends Harvard and then launches his art career in New Orleans with the hopes of making it big enough to return to New York as a painter of significance. "What is probably most remarkable about *The Copper Pot* is what it reveals about Oliver La Farge," McNickle wrote.[18] In particular, McNickle pointed out, the painter's sudden decision to break his engagement to a wealthy New York society woman because he realizes he would lose the freedom to become a serious artist seems poignant when compared to La Farge's decision to marry his first wife.

As La Farge was completing revisions to *The Copper Pot* in December 1941, World War II intervened with the bombing of Pearl Harbor. The following spring, when several thousand soldiers from New Mexico died after being captured at Bataan, La Farge enlisted in the air force, and was promoted during wartime service to lieutenant colonel with the Air Transport Command, in charge of a group of 250 other men. Serving in the military greatly changed La Farge, bringing "a deepening awareness of himself and his relationships to his time and his society" and also giving him a greater self-confidence.[19]

The Man with the Calabash Pipe

Back in Santa Fe, La Farge continued his work as president of the American Association on Indian Affairs, fighting what appeared to be a losing battle to secure Native American rights. The weekly column he began to write in the 1950s for the *Santa Fe New Mexican* covered an astounding array of topics—from the joys and challenges of raising his son (John Pendaries La Farge, born to Consuelo in 1951), to life in a Southwest city. "And [the column] rarely had to do with Indians," his biographer wrote, adding, "All of Santa Fe was his beat, and by turns he scolded, praised, castigated, admired, ridiculed, defended, and obviously loved what he called by turns 'The City Different' and 'The City Difficult,' whose streets are 'very old and hence . . . very tired' and full of ruts."[20] The column ran regularly until La Farge's death in 1963. La Farge's friend, writer Winfield Townley Scott, arranged for some of the columns to be published posthumously in 1966 as *The Man with the Calabash Pipe*, which took its title from a curmudgeonly character who smoked a pipe carved from a gourd shell who appeared in La Farge's columns.

La Farge also established a relationship with the *New Yorker* in the 1950s, which began to publish his short stories about his wife's childhood in Rociada. Mingling fiction with fact, La Farge wrote about the large Baca clan's experiences from the point of view of the Baca children. The stories, collected and published in 1956 as *Behind the Mountain*, debuted in the *New Yorker*, which bought first reading rights to La Farge's work from 1950 to 1962. La Farge also wrote two children's books—the 1953 *Cochise*, a fictionalized biography of the Apache warrior, and *The Mother Ditch*, published in 1954.

Despite ailing health from emphysema, La Farge continued to work as a writer and a Native American rights activist until his death on August 2, 1963. His Pulitzer Prize ensured *Laughing Boy* a place in history and his short stories, though not as well known today, provide a window into authentic Native American cultures of the Southwest. Through his life and work, La Farge forged an intimate connection to the Southwest's Native people, sharing his deep respect for them with readers around the world.

Mural for the Laboratory of Anthropology by William Lumpkin.
Photo by T. Parkhurst. Courtesy Palace of the Governors
(MNM/DCA). Negative no. 74061.

PART TWO

In Taos

[O]nce you have emerged from the canyon of the Rio Grande, you will soon find yourself at Mabel Luhan's having tea with your sybilline hostess and whatever guests may just then be living in the Pink House or the Log Cabin or the Florentine Guest Room— say Thornton Wilder, Myron Brinig or Muriel Draper. Besides Mabel (the most talked of New Mexico writer bar none), you might find Spud Johnson, darkling, slender, and a bit plaintive, either in the office of the Taos Valley News—the local paper which he now edits—or in his Mexican house in Placita, where Laughing Horse, a delightful little magazine—the only one to date printed in this region—is waiting for the depression to lift. From Spud's you would rush on to those high ranches where Frieda Lawrence and Brett abide, and the ghost of D. H. Lawrence still walks. Taos must admit that Lawrence wrote the most clairvoyant pictures of Indian ceremonies ever written in English, as Santa Fe must admit "Death Comes for the Archbishop" as the best novel ever written out of its setting and material.

—Elizabeth Shepley Sergeant,
"The Santa Fe Group"

Mabel Dodge Luhan, 1932. Photo by Will Connell.
Courtesy Palace of the Governors (NMN/DCA). Neg. no. 16755.

CHAPTER SEVEN

Mabel Dodge Luhan

WHILE SANTA FE was remote and isolated in the early 1900s with a population of about seven thousand people, Taos was even more of an outpost, with fewer than two thousand residents. A small village inhabited by Taos Pueblo Indians, descendants of Spanish colonists, and Anglo pioneers, traders, businessmen, and misfits, Taos might seem an odd place to call home for a wealthy socialite with intimate connections to New York and European intellectual circles. Yet Mabel Ganson Evans Dodge Sterne Luhan (whose lengthy name indicates her four marriages) found Taos exhilarating enough to spend more than forty years in an impressive estate she built and named Los Gallos, presiding over luncheons, teas, dinners, and numerous infamous gatherings of the world's elite, including famous writers, painters, photographers, dancers, composers, philosophers, and just about any other intellectual person who had a recognizable name, a good pedigree, or merely the curiosity to "meet Mabel." She lived in Taos almost continuously from her arrival in 1917 until her death in 1962. During her lifetime, this small, plain woman with a mellifluous voice and compelling eyes exerted such a strong influence on the town that visitors and residents alike began referring to it as "Mabeltown."

Luhan, an author, arts patron, activist, and magnet for the world's movers and shakers, invited a diverse group of writers to Taos, hoping that they would share her enthusiasm for the town. She longed to create a counterculture that would thrive because it existed apart from what she viewed as a decaying Western civilization. From the moment she first set foot in Taos in December 1917, Luhan believed she had discovered an exotic world, a "mystical" place she equated with the fabled Atlantis as well as the Far East. This world, she thought, would provide a fabled land where she and her circle of friends could embrace a new way of life. Writing in *Edge of Taos Desert*, the fourth and final volume of her autobiography *Intimate Memories*, Luhan revealed that her "life broke in two" when she arrived in New Mexico "and I entered into the second half, a new world that replaced all the ways I had known with others, more strange and terrible and sweet than any I had ever been able to imagine."[1]

Buffalo Beginnings

Although she was raised in luxurious surroundings, Luhan did not have a happy childhood, according to her biographer Lois Palken Rudnick. Born in 1879 to the Gansons, a wealthy Buffalo family that earned its fortune through banking, she grew up in a strict Victorian household. Her parents offered little nurturing or outward expression of love. Rudnick explained that Luhan's father, Charles Ganson, had studied to be a lawyer but any career had been thwarted by his antisocial behavior and nervous temperament.[2] His wife, Sara Cook Ganson, remained distant from her husband and only child and often took to her bed, where she cried about her loneliness and boredom with life. With such a childhood lacking in attention and love, it is no surprise that Luhan grew up suffering from a desperate need to be loved and a desire to be the center of attention.

Even as a child, Luhan exhibited a strong will and a thirst for life, riding her pony recklessly around her neighborhood, for example, and playing pranks with other children who lived nearby.[3] The adolescent Luhan was, as she later wrote in her memoir, determined to be "joyful, certain, strong."[4] These qualities would later be tempered by bouts of depression that gave way to periods of great activity, "more than most people engage in during a lifetime."[5] This pattern would repeat itself even after Luhan had discovered her paradise in Taos.

Luhan read avidly as a schoolgirl, resonating with works by Byron, Tennyson, Browning, Rosetti, and Matthew Arnold. At age sixteen, she prophetically noted in her poetry journal the opening lines of Arnold's poem "Self-Dependence," which would echo throughout her life: "Weary of myself and sick of asking / What I am, and what I ought to be . . ."[6]

Perhaps such world-weariness propelled Luhan into her first marriage with Karl Evans, following her lavish debut as a society debutante. Evans appealed to her primarily because she thought he already was engaged, and since "she had been emotionally deprived as a child, she believed she had every right to steal love."[7] In 1902, Luhan gave birth to her only child, John, and then immediately stated that she did not want a baby after all. Tellingly, she bore no other children and complications related to the birth forced her to undergo a hysterectomy in 1929. (In 1923, John married the daughter of Santa Fe poet Alice Corbin Henderson and artist, architect, and craftsman William Penhallow Henderson, a union that ended in divorce in 1932 after the couple had three daughters. John tried his hand at writing, producing poetry and two novels—*Andrews' Harvest* [1933] and *Shadows Flying* [1936]—but his work did not impress literary critics.)

The same year that John was born, Luhan's father died. Tragedy struck again in February 1903 when Luhan's husband died after a friend accidentally shot him during a hunting excursion. Luhan, however, did not become the grieving widow. Even before her husband's death, she had started an affair with a prominent married Buffalo doctor who delivered her son and may even have been John's father.[8] Shocked by the scandal, her mother banished Luhan and the infant son to Europe.

European and New York Encounters

On the eve before her Paris-bound ship docked, Luhan met the man who would become her second husband—Edwin Dodge, a well-to-do Bostonian, who had studied architecture at the École des Beaux Arts in Paris. If Luhan had any doubts about whether he might be the right man for her to marry, he convinced her otherwise. The couple wed in October 1904 and soon settled near Florence in an elegant fifteenth-century villa "perched on a hill in Arcetri with a view of Florence and the sweeping roll of land that flattened into the plains leading to Pisa."[9] Ornamented by terraces and gardens heady with the scent of jasmine, gardenias, roses, and olive trees, Luhan easily adopted a regal role. The splendor of Villa Curonia suited her pretensions to "the kind of queen I wanted to be and the type of royal residence in which I would immolate myself,"[10] she wrote in *European Experiences*, the second volume in her four-volume memoir. Rudnick put it this way: "Mabel was like Henry James's Christopher Newman in her American impatience to buy a past that would legitimize her wealth and self."[11]

Luhan put her interior design tastes to work, creating each of the rooms in her villa to reflect her many moods. She decorated the salon, for instance—which stretched more than ninety feet—with heavy tapestries, woven red damask, and rich silk brocades. Her bedroom "was designed like a medieval chamber, complete with a silken ladder that came through a trapdoor above, meant for the rapid descent of a lover . . . Edwin, the ever-practical Bostonian, used the silken ladder only once, to see if it would work."[12] Villa Curonia greatly contrasted with Luhan's Victorian Buffalo home, filled with objects of "drab and deadened sensibilities."[13]

The then current vogue of hosting salons appealed to her, so instead of gathering objects, she began to assemble noteworthy actors, writers, intellectuals, and musicians in her grand salon. Some of the major guests she entertained included author and artist Jacques-Émile Blanche, painter of Nijinsky's portrait, and Leo Stein and his sister, Gertrude Stein, whose salon Luhan had visited during a stay in Paris. When Gertrude Stein visited Luhan in October 1912, she created what became one of her famous writings—"The Portrait of Mabel Dodge Luhan at the Villa Curonia"—while staying at the villa with her partner, Alice B. Toklas. Stein's portrait series, begun in 1908, melded "the raw data of her subject's behavior and attributes and the transforming eye and ear of the artist."[14] For Luhan's portrait, Stein broke new ground in the evolution "of her prose style toward abstraction," apparently inspired by Picasso's synthetic cubism phase. "Well, Pablo is doing abstract portraits in painting. I am trying to do abstract portraits in my medium, words," Stein apparently said.[15] The portrait became famous after being published and handed out at the 1913 New York Armory Show, which Luhan helped promote. She joined on well after the show had already been planned, but her work as a fundraiser and procurer of paintings from private collections became legendary. "Within ten years, she would be credited for hiring her own ocean liner and carting the exhibition over from Europe single-handedly."[16]

One of Stein's lines in the portrait captures Luhan's environs with characteristic candor: "There is the use of the stone and there is the place of the stuff . . . There is the room that is the largest place when there is all that is where there is space."[17] Rudnick offers this interpretation: "It is obvious that Gertrude found in Mabel the kind of discontinuous motion and ever life-renewing energies that she associated with . . . being an American at the dawn of the twentieth century."[18]

Despite her magnificent mansion and luxurious lifestyle, Luhan grew dissatisfied. She felt "that she could not subsist from feeding off of others' lives and loves, or from arranging and rearranging the dead forms of the past."[19] By 1912, having grown bored with Florence and her husband Edwin, she left Europe for New York City. Rudnick theorized that Edwin Dodge initiated the move, hoping to save their marriage after Luhan developed interests in other men. Dodge's maneuvering, however, proved futile. The couple did not divorce until 1916 but their marriage effectively ended shortly after they settled in an apartment in Greenwich Village during the height of the district's avant-garde years. Surrounded by union activists, journalists, and women's rights leaders, Luhan established herself as an integral part of the intellectual scene, hosting heady salons in her apartment in Washington Square starting in January 1913.

Some of the prominent people she traded ideas with included the Steins; journalist Lincoln Steffens; author Walter Lippmann; journalists and fiction writers Max Eastman and Carl Van Vechten; social reformer John Collier; feminists Emma Goldman and Margaret Sanger; photographer and influential gallery owner Alfred Stieglitz, who later married Georgia O'Keeffe; artist Andrew Dasburg; dancer Isadora Duncan; and the revolutionary poet and journalist John Reed, who became her lover. The two met while organizing a pageant for striking silk workers in Paterson, New Jersey, in 1913, and their erratic love affair unraveled after World War I broke out.

In New York, Luhan embraced liberal causes, announcing herself as a radical and a devout supporter of modern art. During this period, she helped promote the influential Armory Show in New York City, which introduced the experimental, post-Impressionist artists of Europe to

Americans, and began writing articles and short stories. Her antiwar article "The Secret of War"—which appeared in the monthly magazine *The Masses* in November 1914—explored through interviews with wounded soldiers and wives of soldiers the "tragic absurdity of young men going to fight in World War I as though they were going to a picnic."[20] Luhan ended her article with the statement that "the only hope of permanent peace lies in a woman's war against war."[21]

Luhan's marriage with Dodge officially ended after she started an affair with the man who would become her third husband: Russian artist Maurice Sterne. To her credit, Luhan sought during that same year to understand the complexity of her uncontrollable mood swings and unquenchable needs. She began treatments in 1916 with A. A. Brill, a follower of Freud who helped start the psychoanalysis movement in America and became her analyst and friend for nearly two decades. Taking Brill's advice, Luhan began to flourish her pen, writing

Mabel Dodge Luhan, date unknown. Courtesy Center for Southwest Research, University Libraries, University of New Mexico. No. 000–494–0779 from the Dorothy Brett Collection.

a syndicated advice column for women that covered topics ranging from sewing quilts to establishing lending libraries and explaining Freudian psychology. Her column discouraging women from submitting to any sort of male authority figure appeared within a week of her marriage to Maurice Sterne, whom she had met the year before in New York City. Sterne had little opportunity to establish any sort of authority over Luhan: within a few months of their marriage, she banished him to the Southwest for eyeing another woman. Her jealousy would soon play a fated role in her future, for Maurice went to New Mexico, from which he sent her a now-famous letter urging her to trek to the Southwest and embrace a new cause, a letter that would completely alter the course of her life.

Summons to Taos

Sterne put Taos on the international map when he sent Luhan the letter, dated November 28, 1917:

> Dearest Girl—Do you want an object in life? Save the Indians, their art—culture—reveal it to the world! . . . for you have energy and are the most sensitive little girl in the world—and above all, there is somehow a strange relationship between yourself and the Indians.[22]

The invitation proved irresistible, and Luhan jumped at the chance to experience Native American culture. She fired back an enthusiastic reply: "Perhaps I too would feel this curious affinity with them that you do. Certainly the live heart of me—the inner life—is a life that finds no counterpart in Western civilization and culture."[23] As she was about to discover, her heart would find its counterpart at Taos Pueblo, and her marriage to a Native American would raise the eyebrows of audiences across America.

Within a few weeks of receiving Sterne's letter, Luhan boarded a train alone and headed to New Mexico to meet her husband as well as her son, who was visiting Sterne in Santa Fe at the time. The journey changed her life. New Mexico instantly appealed to her, but she found Santa Fe overcrowded with people from the East Coast—the kind of people she hoped to escape in New Mexico. In *Edge of Taos Desert*, Luhan wrote about taking an instant dislike to the social scene after attending a tea hosted by artist Paul Burlin and his wife, Natalie Curtis, whose books explored the history of Native American and African American music. One of the guests in attendance, Alice Corbin Henderson, was already a noted poet and editor of the influential *Poetry* magazine. "I don't like it here," Luhan complained to her husband after the tea. "All these people! I want to get *away* somewhere. I don't like living on this *street* and going to *tea parties!*"[24]

In *Edge of Taos Desert*, Luhan explained that a friend's recommendation brought her to Taos. But Henderson's presence must have bothered her. It would, after all, be easier to establish herself in a town that had no successful female poet editing one of America's major literary publications living in it. Whatever reasons brought her there, Luhan felt drawn to Taos from the start, intrigued by its rugged beauty, isolation, and ancient culture. Driving to witness her first Pueblo dance at Santo Domingo Pueblo on the day before Christmas, Luhan received an important insight, recorded in her memoir *Edge of Taos Desert*:

> I had a sudden intuition right then that here in this country, life could come to one more concretely than in other places, and that meanings that were shut up in words and phrases out in the world could incorporate themselves in living forms and move before one. Ideas here might clothe themselves in form and flesh, and word-symbols change into pictured, living realities.[25]

Writing about Taos in the introduction to her 1947 book *Taos and Its Artists*, Luhan further explained her passion for the region by drawing comparisons to the Far East, which poet Witter Bynner also noted:

> This is the provocative landscape that stirs the emotions . . . The landscape that nurtured Lao Tze in China is similar to that one here to which so many artists and writers have opened their hearts. In this high valley there is not a day that does not evoke the emotion of poesy, compounded as the surroundings are of beauty and terror, sun and shadow, revealing almost indefinable subtleties in the golden light and in the abysmal shadows.[26]

Luhan's feelings about Taos were not reciprocated by what some of her neighbors felt about her, especially Arthur Rochford Manby, an eccentric, possibly insane British schemer whose numerous business plans had all failed. Upon deciding to settle in Taos, Luhan rented rooms in an old, dark adobe owned and occupied by Manby, who quickly become suspicious about Luhan's cook, who bore a German last name; her Russian husband; and her frequent visits to Taos Pueblo, which

Nelson Jay, "Tony Luhan at the Gallup, New Mexico Ceremonial," 1938, gelatin silver photograph. Collection of the Museum of Fine Arts, New Mexico. Gift of Nathaniel Owings and Page Allen Owings, 2001.

Manby erroneously believed were all part of a plot to persuade the Pueblo Indians to rise up against America. This was, after all, the World War I era, when all foreigners were suspect. Manby reported Luhan's activities to a federal agent in Albuquerque who traveled to Taos to investigate whether she might be involved in anti-American activities. Manby had assumed that Luhan's belongings, shipped from New York in trunks and boxes, were actually weapons. Luhan relished the attention, for she wrote to a friend that "(w)e are in the maddest, most amusing country in the world—in the freakiest—most insane village you ever dreamed of & I would like to stay forever."[27] She felt worried enough, however, to contact a friend in charge of the federal government's war propaganda unit, the Committee on Public Information, in order to secure her safety.

At the Edge of Taos Desert

Such high drama, coupled with compelling scenery, must have thrilled Luhan, perhaps even encouraged her to discover new depths in her own creativity. As Rudnick noted, Luhan did not find her true voice as a writer until she moved to New Mexico.[28] Tellingly, Rudnick identified *Edge of Taos Desert*, the fourth and final volume of Luhan's memoirs, as the best. "Whereas Mabel is incredibly verbose elsewhere, the language in that book is just stripped bare," Rudnick said during an interview for this book. "She said she wanted to use undomesticated language. I feel that in *Edge of Taos Desert*, she gets what it means to strip things down to the bare bones."[29]

Edge of Taos Desert contains numerous revealing passages, including one describing Mabel's first visit to Taos Pueblo. On this occasion, she met Tony Luhan, a married Taos Pueblo Indian who eventually would leave his Pueblo wife and marry Mabel, despite a Pueblo tradition forbidding intermarriage. (Luhan maintained a deep respect for the traditions of Taos Pueblo, yet when she married Tony seven years later, she altered the spelling of his family name, changing the *j* to an *h* so that her Eastern friends would not mispronounce it.) As she watched Tony wrapped in a blanket and seated by a fireplace, playing a water-drum and singing hypnotically, she longed to shed all of her ties to Western civilization and immerse herself in this undiscovered culture: "I knew I could arrive at this unconscious, full equilibrium, but that

I could only do so by adapting myself," she wrote, adding, "I longed to simply *be* so, as they were, but I knew I must make it for myself as I went along. Not for me, alas, the simple, unthinking harmonies of life; but for me—yes! I thought fiercely—this sumptuous peace and content, this sunny gravity and fire perfume in white-washed walls, at any cost, at any sacrifice."[30] As it turned out, Tony's wife and Luhan's husband became the sacrifices. Once the two fell in love, Luhan sent Sterne back to New York and initiated a divorce, then arranged to pay Tony's wife thirty-five dollars a month for life as long as she agreed to leave the couple alone. Unfortunately, "Mabel herself contracted syphilis from Tony," which later spurred Luhan to launch a campaign to wipe out the venereal disease from Taos Pueblo, starting in 1920, when a Turkish physiologist visiting Luhan discovered that "probably 12 percent of Taos Pueblo had contracted the disease."[31]

Luhan gave up much to move to New Mexico, leaving behind luxury and a large group of sophisticated friends, but she created a new and equally rich lifestyle in Taos. Together, she and Tony created Los Gallos (Spanish for "The Chickens"), an elegant adobe estate built on land adjacent to Taos Pueblo for which Luhan paid fifteen hundred dollars in 1918. The house became a social center for many of the writers, artists, musicians, and intellectuals Luhan invited to Taos.

Los Gallos took its name from the Mexican ceramic chickens painted in vivid colors lining its roof. Tony, who had encouraged her to buy the land, helped Luhan design the building in the Pueblo, or Spanish Revival, architectural style. The look appealed to Luhan because it combined design elements used by the Pueblo people with traditional, natural materials such as wood and adobe (bricks made of mud and straw and baked by the sun). The house's three-story section, for example, echoes Taos Pueblo's multistoried architecture and the high and enclosed sun porch, or solarium, overlooks the four directions held sacred by the Taos Pueblo people. Over the years, the estate grew dramatically. By the time of its completion in the 1930s, Los Gallos contained seventeen rooms, five guesthouses, corrals, stables, barns, and a gatehouse where her servants lived. It remains one of the most famous homes in Taos.

Luhan created the interior spaces of Los Gallos to showcase her extensive world travels and eclectic philosophies. Rudnick described the richly varied decor: "Louis XVI sofas and Second Empire armchairs

Arnold Rönneback, "Casa Luhan, Taos," 1925, watercolor on paper.
Collection of the Museum of Fine Arts, New Mexico. Museum
purchase and donation from the estate of Arnold Rönneback, 2003.

shared space with Cedar Rapids oak and pine trestle tables; straw-seated Mexican chairs with bentwood chairs, seated Buddhas with standing Virgins, Navajo rugs with French silk wall hangings."[32]

From Los Gallos, Luhan continued to address the world with hopes that by educating others about Pueblo religion, art, and fertile connections to land, the "barbaric" Western race could be saved. She brought the world's intellectual and artistic elite to Taos, encouraging them to write about the role that Pueblo Indians could play in saving Western civilization from its rotting core. She described the Pueblo people as "time-binders" who could reveal the "power of life" to the white culture.[33]

The Weight of the Bursum Bill

Luhan also became an ardent proponent of Native American rights. She played a huge part in defeating the Bursum Bill, introduced in Congress in 1922 by a U.S. senator from New Mexico, Holm Olaf Bursum, as an attempt to settle a long-standing property dispute between two groups who claimed to own the same land—Pueblo Indians and non-Pueblo "squatters." The bill proposed to give clear title to any non-Pueblo residents who could prove they owned a title dating to at least 1902.

The legislation outraged Native American activists around the country, who believed that once again the U.S. government blatantly sought to steal land that belonged to Native Americans. Reaction was swift. The General Federation of Women's Clubs, which had an Indian Welfare Committee, took sides with the Pueblos and launched a fight against the bill with help from progressive social reformer John Collier—who became the commissioner of Indian Affairs in 1933 and crafted the Indian New Deal to protect Native American culture and provide a stable economy for America's indigenous people. Luhan and Collier were friends. She persuaded him to visit Taos so he could have his first encounter with Native American life on the pueblos. He and his family stayed at Los Gallos during their visit to New Mexico, and he joined Luhan in waging a fierce battle to defeat the Bursom Bill. This was, after all, what Luhan had come to Taos to do—help save the Indians!

Luhan enlisted national support for the Protest of Artists and Writers Against the Bursum Bill, signed by other writers of the Santa Fe and Taos colonies. She persuaded D. H. Lawrence to write an article against the bill that appeared in the *New York Times*. Alice Corbin Henderson, Mary Austin, and journalist Elizabeth Shepley Sergeant also wrote articles for the same cause, and Austin gave a speech in Washington to the National Popular Government League, an urban reform group. Tony also joined the battle. The protestors' hard work paid off with the bill's defeat in January 1923. But the national uproar threatened to put Luhan in an uncomfortable spotlight regarding her relationship with Tony, who was then still married to his Taos Pueblo wife. Austin and others encouraged Mabel to marry Tony and make their relationship official before the government could expose their affair, causing negative publicity.

When Luhan and Tony finally married on April 23, 1923, the nuptials made the national news. Newspapers treated the event disparagingly, carrying headlines such as the one in the *Pittsburgh Post*: "Why Bohemia's Queen Married an Indian Chief."[34] Luhan mistakenly believed the publicity would further her cause to promote Pueblo culture: Rudnick cited an interview Luhan gave to the *Colorado Post* nine years after her marriage, in which she expressed the hope that other marriages between Native Americans and whites would follow hers so that "the races may amalgamate and the Indians be the ones to save our race."[35]

Luhan and Collier continued their fight for Native American rights into the 1930s, when Collier launched the Indian New Deal. She also kept up her crusade to bring the world's elite to Taos so that they too could enjoy the unique beauty and culture of the land she now called home.

CHAPTER EIGHT

D. H. Lawrence in Taos

THE MOST SIGNIFICANT writer Mabel Dodge Luhan lured to Taos was the famous British author D. H. Lawrence. Having read much of his work, including his autobiographical novel *Sons and Lovers*, she believed that this slight, red-haired, moody man was the one writer in the world who could produce the book she desperately wanted written about the deep mysteries of the Taos landscape and Pueblo life. As she wrote in her 1934 memoir *Lorenzo in Taos*, Lawrence "is the only one who can really see this Taos country and the Indians, and who can describe it so that it is as much alive between the covers of a book as it is in reality."[1]

The Search for Paradise

Seeking an appropriate place to establish a utopian community he called Rananim (a word meaning "celebrations" borrowed from a Hebrew folk song), Lawrence responded to Mabel's invitation to come to Taos and see a place "like the dawn of the world," as she described it in a letter to him in 1921.[2] At the time he received the letter, Lawrence was en route to America, journeying through India, Ceylon, and Australia, places where his encounters with the "dark" races "had brought out his latent racist paranoia."[3] He anticipated visiting America's Southwest

D. H. Lawrence outside Witter Bynner's house, 1922 or 1923.
Courtesy The Witter Bynner Foundation for Poetry.

because he believed its indigenous culture offered him a chance to "shift American consciousness toward organic expression," which existed in Native American life.[4] In his essay "America, Listen to Your Own," Lawrence explained his philosophy: "Americans must take up life where the Red Indian, the Aztec, the Maya, the Incas left it off . . . They must catch the pulse of life which Cortes and Columbus murdered. There lies the real continuity; not between Europe and the new States, but between the murdered Red America and the seething White America."[5]

Lawrence arrived in Taos with his German wife, Frieda, in September 1922, armed with great hopes about what he might find at Taos Pueblo. In Lawrence's oft-quoted 1928 essay "New Mexico," published in 1936 in Lawrence's *Phoenix: The Posthumous Papers*, he shared his first happy impressions: I think New Mexico was the greatest experience from the outside world that I have ever had . . . The moment I saw the brilliant, proud morning shine high up over the deserts of Santa Fe, something stood still in my soul and I started to attend."[6] But by the end of his third and final visit from March to September 1925, Lawrence had firmly decided that he did not share Luhan's fervent belief that Taos Pueblo culture would save the American race. His essay "Just back from the Snake-Dance—Tired Out," published in *Laughing Horse* magazine, made clear Lawrence's opinions about the effects of the white culture's encroachment on Indian culture:

The southwest is the great playground of the White American. The desert isn't good for anything else. But it does make a fine national playground. And the Indian with his long hair and his bits of pottery and blankets and clumsy home-made trinkets, he's a wonderful live toy to play with. More than keeping rabbits, and just as harmless. Wonderful, really, hopping round with a snake in his mouth. Lots of fun! Oh, the wild west is lots of fun; The Land of Enchantment. Like being right inside the circus ring![7]

Lawrence believed that Luhan, in trying to save the Indians, was really only "using what she learned about Indian life to strengthen and market her own ego."[8] He felt hemmed in by Luhan's hunger to manipulate people and events, a trait he equated with the character of American culture. As Rudnick asserted, Luhan "became for Lawrence the incarnation of evil that was masked by America's benevolent will. American benevolence, as he well understood, had a way of making dependents of the less fortunate others it felt morally bound to liberate as a means of affirming its sacred 'mission.'"[9]

A Fractured Friendship

Lawrence had no patience for Luhan's domineering will and her demands to control the subjects he wrote about. According to Rudnick, each hinted that the other had attempted seduction, but it seems unlikely that a physical relationship took place since each considered the other to be "physically repellent." Lawrence, in fact, felt so uncomfortable with the uncovered second-story bathroom windows in Los Gallos that he painted the glass, covering it with vivid designs perhaps to avoid having to see Luhan naked as much as to prevent others from seeing him in the same state.

Nonetheless, Lawrence's initial visit began well. Luhan felt that Lawrence shared her passion for the power of words and they bonded over a collaborative project, a book about Luhan's life, which she desperately wanted Lawrence to write. But a bitter rivalry soon erupted between Luhan and Lawrence's wife, Frieda, who believed that Luhan cared nothing about collaborating with Lawrence and wanted only to dominate him and use him to her own devices. For her part, Luhan resented Frieda's ease with her own sexuality and her intimate connection to Lawrence. Characteristically Lawrence balked, growing increasingly repelled as he realized why Luhan had lured him to New Mexico. As Luhan described it, "I wanted to seduce his spirit so that I could make him carry out certain things . . . It was his soul I needed for my purpose, his soul, his will, his creative imagination, and his lighted vision."[10]

Some aspects of Luhan's complicated personality worked like a muse on Lawrence. As Rudnick pointed out, "Mabel's quest for spiritual and emotional redemption became the central theme of his American fiction."[11] Rudnick cited Lawrence scholar L. D. Clark's observation that during Lawrence's visits to America, he became "absorbed in the theme of the woman in search and made it the dominant one in every important piece of fiction that he wrote from the inspiration of this continent."[12] Clark's point is underscored in Lawrence's acclaimed short story "The Woman Who Rode Away," in which the bored wife of a miner in Mexico seeks adventure and ends up being ritually sacrificed by a remote tribe of Indians. Indeed, in the title character of the story, we see a strong will and desire to seek otherness—traits that Luhan possessed and that undoubtedly gave Lawrence inspiration for his doomed character. Writing this story, which ends with the heroine's death, must have given Lawrence the opportunity to vent the anger Luhan sparked in him. It also allowed him to draw from his experiences witnessing Native American ceremonies and dances in northern New Mexico as inspiration for the Mexican Indian ceremonials he described in this story.

As frustrated as he was by Luhan's desire to dominate, Lawrence considered extending her an invitation to join his utopian colony, which remained an unfulfilled vision. With her participation in Rananim in mind, he convinced her to dress according to his whim, changing her style from loosely draped garments to "Mother Hubbard" dresses paired with "white stockings and aprons with hair ribbons to match, a get-up which made Mabel look like an overgrown Alice-in-Wonderland."[13] He also persuaded her to cook and clean house, chores she'd never done before and, as Lawrence discovered, could not perform with any grace. Her willingness to make these changes for Lawrence indicated just how much she wanted to please him.

By November, though, Lawrence had endured enough. Wanting to escape Luhan and her constant need to control him, he and Frieda moved seventeen miles away from Los Gallos and into a primitive cabin on the Del Monte Ranch, situated north of Taos. They invited two Danish painters who were visiting Taos to stay with them at the ranch. One of these painters, Knud Merrild, wrote *A Poet and Two Painters*, a memoir about his acquaintance with Lawrence published in 1938. To Merrild, Lawrence revealed the extent of his rage at Luhan, swearing that he wished to murder her. Lawrence also conveyed his anger in a letter to Frieda's mother, saying that Luhan "wants to be a witch and at the same time Mary of Bethany at Jesus' feet—a big, white crow, a cooing raven of ill-omen, a little buffalo."[14]

The Lawrences remained ensconced in the cabin on Del Monte Ranch until March 1923, when they took a trip to Mexico with poet Witter

Bynner and his secretary and companion Spud Johnson. During this trip, Lawrence wrote the first draft of *Quetzalcoatl*, which he later revised as *The Plumed Serpent*. He cast Bynner and Johnson as two minor characters in the novel (see chapter 3).

At Kiowa Ranch

When Lawrence and his wife returned to New Mexico for a second stay from March through October 1924, he felt ready to establish a productive and peaceful friendship with Luhan. Despite their differences, they had formed a relationship that "was never completely severed."[15] But by May, the friendship between Lawrence and Luhan began to sour once again. The tension drove the Lawrences to move into a run-down, three-room ranch that Luhan had purchased for her son, about seventeen miles north of Taos. Lawrence called the property Lobo Ranch, then later Kiowa Ranch, after an old Native American trail that ran through the property. Through Frieda, Luhan arranged to give the Lawrences the ranch in exchange for Lawrence's manuscript of *Sons and Lovers*. Still, the relationship between Lawrence and Luhan never achieved an easy balance. Luhan last saw Lawrence in the autumn of 1924 before he and Frieda left for Mexico, and though they had a cordial parting, she soon learned from friends whom the Lawrences had visited in Santa Fe before their departure that he had described her as "hopeless," "destructive," and "dangerous."[16] "I gave up Lawrence then," Luhan wrote in *Lorenzo in Taos*, adding, "That is, I gave up expectation, so far as he was concerned, and I wrote him a letter on the train as the land and rivers widened between us. I told him it was no use, no use at all, to believe in him, friendship, his affection or even his actuality. I told him he was incapable of friendship or loyalty—and that his core was treacherous."[17]

When the Lawrences returned for their third and final visit to New Mexico, staying at Kiowa Ranch from April to September 1925, they avoided visiting Luhan altogether. Lawrence, however, continued to write to her, and before his death at age forty-four from tuberculosis in France in 1930, the two seemed to have ended their feud. Indeed, in letters Lawrence wrote to Luhan from France before he died, he suggested they might "begin a new life, with real tenderness in it." His early death robbed them both of that possibility, but judging by their past experiences, a peaceful relationship seemed unlikely.[18]

Lawrence's Legacies

After Lawrence's death, Luhan sent Frieda a rough draft of her memoir of the great British author, *Lorenzo in Taos*. According to Lawrence's biographer Brenda Maddox, Frieda was upset that Luhan had "emphasized the comic elements of their life in Taos at the expense of the spiritual, and made it seem as if they all had been playing a game of charades."[19] Frieda shot back with an autobiography of her own, *Not I, But the Wind*, published in 1934. Frieda clearly wanted to paint a more positive portrait of Lawrence, and her book offered a romantic and emotional account of their marriage. Both books contained private letters each author had received from Lawrence.

Frieda returned to Taos from Europe in 1933 with her lover Angelo Ravagli, an Italian lieutenant from whom she and Lawrence had rented a villa in Spotorno, Italy. (The couple married in 1950, after U.S. immigration officials began to question the validity of their relationship.) They took up residence at Kiowa Ranch. But, according to Frieda Lawrence's biographer Robert Lucas, Ravagli found the cabin too rustic, so he built a house with running water and electricity to provide Frieda with a more comfortable life than she had experienced living there with Lawrence. He also built a little chapel on a hill near the cabin to hold Lawrence's ashes.

Lawrence had been buried in Vence, France, where he died, but Frieda later decided to exhume his body, have him cremated, and then bring his ashes to New Mexico, believing it was what he would have wanted. Frieda's decision, as her biographer pointed out, mirrored Lawrence's own enduring fascination with the phoenix, the mythical bird possessing the ability to rise from death, reborn from its own ashes. Lawrence's own ashes became the stuff of legend as well.

According to Frieda's biographer Lucas, Ravagli journeyed to Vence in 1934 to have the cremation carried out. After visiting his family in Europe, Ravagli returned in April 1935 carrying Lawrence's ashes. But he was detained in New York by U.S. immigration officials who had not forgotten that Lawrence's famous novel *Lady Chatterley's Lover* had been banned after its publication in 1928 because of its sex scenes and language. Lucas explained that it took "lengthy negotiations and intervention from above" for Ravagli to bring the "precious urn" onto American soil.[20]

From there, events became even more complicated. Frieda and a group of friends apparently met Ravagli at the train station in Lamy. Then, while listening to his story in a Lamy bar, they drank too much, or became distracted by Ravagli's narrative. Perhaps both events contributed to the confusion. Whatever the reason, the group drove away, leaving the urn on the station platform. Realizing their error, they returned to reclaim it and then headed up to Taos, where they stopped to visit an artist in whose studio the urn was once again forgotten. The next day, according to Lucas, the urn was retrieved. That, at least, is one version of the truth. Other accounts blamed Ravagli for leaving the ashes on the train, never to be recovered. But that seems less likely in light of events that reportedly ensued.

Frieda's biographer explained that once Lawrence's ashes had made it safely into Frieda's hands, the volatile friendship she had with Luhan erupted. Luhan wanted to scatter the ashes across the Kiowa Ranch

Mabel Dodge, Frieda Lawrence, and Dorothy Brett,
from left to right, date unknown. Courtesy Sunstone Press.

property, but Frieda wanted to hold a sunset ceremony for family and friends to place the urn in the chapel built by Ravagli. Firmly believing that Lawrence wanted his ashes strewn across the Kiowa Ranch property, Luhan tried to control events by staging an elaborate stunt. She planned to have artist Dorothy Brett, Lawrence's devoted friend, who was painting glass in the chapel, steal the urn so that Luhan could carry out her own wishes. Frieda, however, had learned of Luhan's plot and she fought back, informing Luhan that she had uncovered her scheme and then making sure the urn remained under watch. The sunset ceremony took place with a ritual Pueblo dance, which Luhan did not attend. She did, however, send a letter to Frieda, warning that once Frieda was dead, Luhan would ensure that Lawrence's ashes were scattered as she saw fit. Frieda's response was to ensure that Luhan would never be able to carry this out. She told Ravagli to mix the ashes with sand and cement into an altar block that remains in the chapel today. Lawrence, it seems, was one of the few people who could outdo Luhan in death as well as in life.

Frieda Lawrence died in 1956 at age seventy-seven, having never developed a stable friendship with Luhan. (Most people who came within Luhan's orbit found it hard to get along with her for long periods of time.) The relationship between these two women, however, was complicated by yet another female presence in Taos whose life intersected Lawrence's: Dorothy Brett, an eccentric, aristocratic Englishwoman and the only friend of Lawrence's who took up his offer to leave England to join his utopia.

Brett accompanied the Lawrences during their second sojourn to Taos in 1924 as Lawrence's faithful supporter. During their stays at Kiowa Ranch, Brett tolerated life in a tiny cabin on the property simply to be near the man she considered a genius. Hard of hearing, she carried around an ear trumpet nicknamed "Toby" and often yelled at others, which frequently frustrated Luhan. She irked Frieda, too, who complained that Brett tagged along because she was in love with her husband. While rivalry could bitterly divide Luhan and Frieda, their mutual impatience with Brett was one thing that brought them together. After Lawrence's death, Brett stayed on in Taos until her death in 1977, outliving the two women with whom she had been cast in the complicated triangle of female power that surrounded Lawrence in Taos.

CHAPTER NINE

Mabel Dodge Luhan, After D. H. Lawrence

WITH D. H. LAWRENCE gone and the ultimate book about Taos still unwritten, Mabel Dodge Luhan turned to poet Robinson Jeffers, hoping he could "give a voice to this speechless land," as she wrote in *Lorenzo in Taos*.[1] At Luhan's invitation, Jeffers and his family began to spend summers in Taos in the 1930s.

Jeffers and Luhan first met in Carmel in 1930, when Jeffers was widely considered America's greatest living poet. Luhan became convinced that Jeffers could accomplish what Lawrence did not: write fervently about the culture of the Pueblo Indians. Jeffers, however, "believed that the Pueblos had nothing to offer Anglos because they were too contaminated by their civilization."[2]

One more time, Luhan felt the need to play muse to a great writer. She failed yet again, this time with more disastrous consequences. In 1937, when Jeffers was in the throes of a severe depression brought on by writer's block, Luhan blamed his wife, Una, and decided to take drastic, nearly fatal action. "Once again, she felt called upon to save a great artist from his wife," her biographer Lois Palken Rudnick explained.[3] Luhan encouraged an affair between Jeffers and a young woman visiting her that summer. When Una Jeffers discovered her husband's betrayal, she tried to take her own life. Typically, the self-absorbed Luhan refused to see how her own actions brought about the tragedy.

Instead, she coldly blamed Una Jeffers for refusing to accept the fact that an affair might have helped to quell her husband's depression.

Writing a Life

Despite her bad behavior, Luhan established a national reputation as the "first lady" of Taos, having worked hard to publicize the beauty of Taos, secure Native American rights, and alert the rest of the country about the mystical power of Pueblo culture during the 1920s. The 1930s ushered in a new role for her as hardworking author of a lengthy memoir, *Intimate Memories*, consisting of four volumes—*Background*, *European Experiences*, *Movers and Shakers*, and *Edge of Taos Desert*—published in 1933, 1935, 1936, and 1937, respectively. During his time in Taos, and even from elsewhere in letters he sent to Luhan, Lawrence played a significant role in persuading Luhan to write about her own life.

Tony Luhan and Mabel Dodge Luhan, date unknown. Courtesy Center for Southwest Research, University Libraries, University of New Mexico. No. 000-494-2402 from the Dorothy Brett Collection.

For a model, however, Luhan looked to Marcel Proust's *Remembrance of Things Past*, "in which sin, selfishness, pride, and envy abound in the hero's allegorical search for truth and redemption," Rudnick explained.[4] She took more than ten years to complete her memoir.

The first volume fared poorly with many literary critics, who felt it reflected Luhan's narcissism. "Nor were they taken by her subject matter, her hyperbolic style, or her romantic sensibility," Rudnick wrote.[5] *Edge of Taos Desert*, however, received a warmer reception, most likely because the language and style were different from that which she had employed in the three other volumes of her memoir. "Her final volume focuses our attention on the stripping away of her civilized veneer," Rudnick wrote.[6] Photographer Ansel Adams, who spent time in one of Luhan's guesthouses in the summer of 1930, wrote to Luhan that *Edge of Taos Desert* would encourage people to "'take life with the talons' and carry it high."[7]

More Noteworthy Visitors

Luhan took time off from writing her memoirs to entertain other significant people who visited Taos after Lawrence, including painter Georgia O'Keeffe, who visited Luhan during the summer of 1929 and felt an instant rapport with the landscape. During the 1930s, Luhan's guest list expanded to include musician Leopold Stokowski and author Thomas Wolfe. Stokowski, considered one of America's greatest musicians at the time, arrived in 1932 to hear and record the music of Taos Pueblo, but was unable to create high quality recordings. He returned briefly in 1934 and was the guest of honor at a dinner feast at Taos Pueblo.

Playwright and novelist Thornton Wilder, the only writer to win Pulitzer prizes for both literature and drama, also trekked to Taos to visit Luhan. He gave a guest lecture at the Taos Open Forum during the winter of 1933–34. He and Luhan became good friends, and Wilder looked to Luhan for literary criticism and support. Wilder, though, had little patience for the gossip and rivalries that frequently characterized the Santa Fe and Taos writers' colonies, a trait he would reveal in his revered play *Our Town*, which debuted in 1938. During one of his forays to Taos in the fall of 1934, he attended a dinner party where Santa Fe poet Witter Bynner made fun of the local literary scene. Wilder surely knew about the feud between his Taos hostess and Bynner, sparked by Bynner's derogatory portrayal of Luhan in his play *Cake: An Indulgence*. He might merely have wanted to assure Luhan that he was on her side when he reported to her that he had challenged Bynner after listening to his jokes, "that the portrait of the portraitist that emerged from the portrait is even more unlovely than the sitter."[8] Then again, perhaps Wilder was simply insulted by the petty gossip, not understanding how rooted it was in the northern New Mexico literary colonies.

Novelist Thomas Wolfe journeyed to Taos at Luhan's request, but his visit in July 1935 turned out to be "Mabel's most magnificent failure."[9] On his way to Luhan's house for dinner, he stopped in Santa Fe to attend a lunch held expressly for him. The celebration continued in a car ride to Taos accompanied by two women he met at the lunch, and by the time he arrived at Luhan's house, he was totally drunk. She refused to see him, even though she greatly admired his writing.

Myron Brinig and *The Taos Truth Game*

When Myron Brinig first came to Taos in 1933, he was then widely considered one of America's rising literary stars by readers and critics alike. A Jewish novelist born in 1896, he grew up in Butte, Montana, and wrote twenty-one novels before his death in 1991. Much of his fiction realistically portrayed the hardships of miners, labor activists, farmers, and other figures connected to America's pioneer era. One of his novels became the basis for the 1938 Warner Brothers' film *The Sisters*, starring Bette Davis and Errol Flynn.

"Brinig was one of the earliest Jewish novelists writing in English about Jewish immigrants," wrote Earl Ganz in his afterword to *The Taos Truth Game*, his fascinating novel about Brinig's experiences in northern New Mexico, primarily during the 1930s.[10] "Only the gay critics are beginning to deal with him. Brinig was the first writer from the West to write about being gay."[11]

When Ganz tracked down Brinig in 1981, a few years after discovering his work in the University of Montana library, the author was living in New York City, utterly forgotten by the world. Attempting to revive an interest in Brinig's work, Ganz convinced Montana's Historical Society to reprint Brinig's 1931 labor novel *Wide Open Town*, based on the 1917 copper strike against Anaconda Copper Company and the lynching of a union organizer. The society reissued the novel in 1991 as part of its reprint series devoted to writers of Montana. Three months before the publication date, though, Brinig died at age ninety-four. He left behind two drafts of memoir, "Love from a Stranger," which he and Ganz had edited "so it would stress the years he lived in Taos, my thought being that because he had known so many famous people there, it would be interesting to publishers."[12]

Brinig's final published book appeared in 1958 when he was sixty-one. One of his best books, according to Ganz, is *You and I*. This 1941 novel offers a retelling of Brinig's favorite fairy tale, *Hansel and Gretel*, with the title characters cast as adopted siblings who eventually fall in love. The story begins in Taos, and shifts to Butte and then New York City before winding up back in Taos.

Brinig first saw Taos in the spring of 1933 during a cross-country driving trip to Los Angeles from New York City. He fell immediately in love with the region as well as with painter Cady Wells, then living near Taos. Their relationship ended in 1938, and Brinig then bought Luhan's Placita property, next to Spud Johnson's house, a historic adobe Luhan and Tony occupied while building Los Gallos. After moving out, the couple had used it as a guesthouse for various visitors including D. H. Lawrence, Frieda, and Ansel Adams, who was still considering a career as a concert pianist when he stayed with Luhan during the summers of 1929 and 1930. Brinig sold the house in 1954, after Wells died suddenly and prematurely of a heart attack, presumably because of what he experienced after enlisting as a U.S. soldier and fighting with General Patton's army in Germany and Normandy, France, during World War II.

Before Brinig's death, Ganz traveled to New York to meet him in his midtown apartment and discuss his life. That was when Brinig shared his unedited memoirs, a work-in-progress called "Love from a Stranger." He told Ganz that the idea for the tentative title arose from a phrase once uttered by silent film director D. W. Griffith.

The Taos Truth Game offers a fascinating look into the writers' era in Santa Fe as well as in Taos, and while Ganz wrote it as a novel, he drew some of the scenes directly from Brinig's memoirs, which may have been embellished too.

Winter in Taos

Despite her busy life, Luhan continued to write, and in 1935 *Winter in Taos* was published. Rudnick considered it Luhan's "finest literary work, the one that comes closest to sustaining the richly integrated sense of self and environment, form and content, that she hoped the writers she brought to celebrate Taos would achieve."[13] She patterned the book after the cycles of seasons and life on Taos Pueblo. Though it takes place during a single winter day, Luhan explores memories of other seasons, examining the notion of solitude and extolling the ability of the earth to renew itself daily as well as seasonally. Two years later, she finished *Edge of Taos Desert*, in which she revealed in one of the later chapters that, despite her disapproval of Tony's taking peyote as part of a Taos Pueblo ritual, she took it too. She explained that Tony persuaded her to believe it could help her recover quickly from a sudden illness that set in after she got caught in the rain during an overnight outing on horses in the Taos mountains with Tony and friends. Much to her delight, she completely enjoyed the altered experience.

Not long after the publication of *Edge of Taos Desert*, Luhan spiraled into a midlife crisis that she feared indicated a loss of creativity. The cure involved returning to New York and resuming sessions with her therapist, A. A. Brill, who helped her to revive interest in her life's work. Over the next decade, Luhan spent time in New York, where she launched another salon that lasted just a few weeks. She also wrote an unpublished novel that Rudnick called her worst failure at fiction. In her final book, *Taos and Its Artists*, published in 1947, Luhan celebrated the painters who had captured the land she so loved, describing Taos as "a fabulous honeycomb, irresistible and nourishing."[14]

The Final Years

Taos, however, was beginning a major change, propelled in part by the work that Luhan and her friends had undertaken to promote it. America had discovered the tiny town, and tourists began to flock to see the landscape and culture they had read so much about. Before her death on August 13, 1962, Luhan began to lament the transformation of Taos into what she called "Tinsel Land." She bemoaned the arrival of tourists intent on seeking out thrills, rather than the artists and writers she had invited to celebrate the cultural diversity of the region. As early as the 1940s, she began to consider leaving Taos for good. She stayed, though, even as her health declined. Growing older, she experienced bouts of senility worsened by a propensity for alcohol. She had several strokes in the 1950s but lived on until 1962, when she died of a coronary thrombosis. Her husband, Tony, died the following year. Although Luhan's difficult personality had not made her popular with many Taos residents, she had taken steps to improve the community, financing a hospital and a bandstand, and donating to the Harwood Foundation, a community art and culture center, her collection of *santos* (painted and carved images of saints) and thousands of books.

Luhan is buried in the Kit Carson Historic Cemetery in the center of Taos not far from her famous home, which is now an inn. Little has changed at Los Gallos, and the estate retains the atmosphere of Luhan's heyday. According to the inn's employees, her spirit haunts the property. Her modest grave in the cemetery's southwest corner seems small when compared to the giant role she played in establishing the literary colony based in Taos whose legacies have reached well beyond New Mexico's borders.

CHAPTER TEN

Spud Johnson

IF MABEL DODGE LUHAN stood sternly at the center of the Taos literary colony during the 1920s and 1930s, Walter Willard Johnson, known to all as "Spud," occupied a prominent, more playful spot, not just in Taos but also in Santa Fe. Without this slight, witty, and often self-deprecating man, life in the writers' colonies would have been neither as amusing nor as chronicled as it was. Johnson was a poet, an expert printer, and one of the founders of *Laughing Horse*, a little magazine that traveled far in the world, poking fun at politics, literature, and a host of other subjects. Although it was small, *Laughing Horse* published some of the most important writers of its time. Johnson also penned a book of poems along with hundreds of columns for local and national publications about life in Santa Fe and Taos. He also created his own weekly one-page newspaper in Taos called *The Horse Fly*, subtitled the "Smallest and Most Inadequate Newspaper Ever Published." He may have been small in stature and quiet around others, but his voice thundered across the country, thanks to his printing press and his wit with words.

Formative Years

When Johnson was born in 1897 in Illinois, ink surely coursed through his blood. From an early age, he knew he wanted to write, according to

Willard "Spud" Johnson, date unknown. Courtesy Harwood Museum of Art of the University of New Mexico. No. 997.82.

his biographer Sharyn R. Udall, author of *Spud Johnson & Laughing Horse*. His family moved to Greeley, Colorado, when he was nine years old, and there he began his journalism career, founding and editing his high school newspaper and writing for the local newspaper. He briefly studied at the University of Colorado in Boulder before heading to Berkeley, California, in 1920, seeking an environment populated with writers and other intellectuals.

While taking classes at the University of California, he met Witter

Bynner, an established poet teaching at the university. Bynner, who belonged to a fashionable Bay Area literary circle, introduced Johnson to other noted writers and encouraged him to write poetry. Their friendship became intimate and, when Bynner settled in Santa Fe, he invited Johnson to visit him. Johnson arrived in the summer of 1922 and quickly decided to become a resident of northern New Mexico, joining the group of writers intent on informing the rest of America about the region's ancient culture, beautiful landscape, and exotic appeal.

Laughing Horse Takes Off

Before leaving Berkeley, Johnson launched a venture that would dominate his life for nearly two decades. With just fifty dollars of his savings, he and two other students he met in a literature class—Roy Chanslor and James Van Rensselaer Jr.—started the monthly magazine at the university on April 10, 1922, promising in the inaugural edition to ridicule "everything which seems to us to affect too pontifical an air, too solemn an attitude . . ."[1] They added that Laughing Horse was intended as "a healthful reaction to the whole timid, vacillating conservative spirit which now prevails over this land," and explained that they sought to offer "a robust skepticism" and to "have our fun and our chuckles and we hope that you will, too."[2]

Johnson's biographer pointed out that the editors "were self-appointed satirists of almost everything," offering up servings of literary as well as social criticism, "mocking the perceived 1920s domination of American culture by the middle class."[3] Their skill at skewering the mainstream literary and social issues of the day became immediately evident in the first two issues published in the spring of 1922, which caught the attention of regional newspapers that ran laudatory articles about the new magazine. Officials at the University of California did not share the enthusiasm, but by then Johnson was safely ensconced in Santa Fe and thus avoided certain expulsion.

Taking on Censorship

Laughing Horse stampeded straight into trouble with its fourth issue. Having met D. H. Lawrence when the famed British writer and his wife came to Taos to visit Mabel Dodge Luhan in 1922, Johnson convinced

Cover of *Laughing Horse*, December 1923.
Courtesy Gerald Peters Gallery Bookstore.

Lawrence to write a piece for the magazine. The British author turned in a highly negative book review of Ben Hecht's novel *Fantazius Mallare*. Lawrence's review, crafted as a letter to America's youth, vehemently expressed his dislike of Hecht's writing style and subject matter using some highly unsavory language, which the editors decided to replace with dashes. As Johnson's biographer noted, university officials were "deeply shocked; it seemed a clear act of provocation by Johnson and his co-editors, a move calculated to test, and perhaps embarrass, administration officials, who instantly declared the letter obscene and suspended publication of the magazine."[4] *Laughing Horse*'s predicament, however, only brought more attention to the little magazine, and the topic of censorship became a major issue in its pages for years to come.

The university decided to charge *Laughing Horse* with publishing obscene matter, but officials undoubtedly took additional offense at the editorial decision to excerpt, in the same edition, parts of Upton Sinclair's new book, *The Goose Step: A Study of American Education.* In such chapters as "The Dean of Imperialism," "The Drill Sergeant on the Campus," and "The Fortress of Medievalism," Sinclair exposed what he considered to be corrupt politics at the University of California.[5] The university ignored Sinclair's accusations, but officials took further action by expelling Chanslor, the only editor still registered at the university as a student, and bringing him to trial on the charge of printing obscene matter. The case was dismissed, but not before it helped *Laughing Horse* gain even more recognition in the avant-garde and academic worlds.

Laughing Horse Heads to the Southwest

With Johnson settled in the Southwest, *Laughing Horse* began to reflect more of the region, carrying articles by many Santa Fe and Taos writers as well as illustrations by prominent members of the Santa Fe and Taos art colonies. Bynner, an advocate for the magazine from its inception, contributed poetry and articles, including the Spectra poetry he had written under the pseudonym Emanuel Morgan. Other Santa Fe contributors during this time included author Mary Austin, poet Haniel Long, and poet and playwright Lynn Riggs.

Political issues of the day concerning the Southwest began to receive attention as well in *Laughing Horse.* In the fifth issue, Johnson's brief article "Poets and Indians in Politics" informed readers about the successful defeat of the Bursum Bill, largely because of the opposition effort led by Mabel Dodge Luhan and her friend, progressive social reformer John Collier—who became the commissioner of Indian Affairs in 1933. The opposition movement included outspoken support against the bill from writers, artists, and others around the country. In his article,

Cover of *Laughing Horse*, April 1926, with D. H. Lawrence's portrait.
Courtesy Gerald Peters Gallery Bookstore.

Johnson pointed out with characteristic wit that a "succinct and naïve"
letter sent by residents of Acoma Pueblo argued the point much better
than the "manifesto of all these noted writers."[6]

Even with all the publicity, *Laughing Horse*, which sold for twenty-five
cents (or "two bits"), struggled with financial difficulties. It started as a

monthly magazine yet only appeared nine times during its first twenty months. The financial challenges of publication affected Johnson's coeditors, who soon developed other professional and personal interests. Johnson, however, remained committed to the venture, certain that he could publish *Laughing Horse* from the Southwest. He realized that the magazine could fulfill "a real need for New Mexico writers, most of whom had to publish outside the region to be published at all."[7] He took on primary responsibilities, from writing and soliciting contributions to printing the magazine and later selling advertisements, for which he wrote the copy. He even contributed some of his own whimsical art to accompany original illustrations by many of the Santa Fe and Taos artists. The burden of putting out the magazine single-handedly forced Johnson to publish *Laughing Horse* quarterly instead of monthly, a decision that he announced in the ninth issue.

Laughing Horse often traveled with Johnson as well. When he journeyed to Mexico in 1923 with the Lawrences and Witter Bynner, for example, the eighth issue was devoted to Mexico and printed in Guadalajara by a local printer. During the winter of 1925–26, while Johnson visited Mabel Dodge Luhan during her stay in Croton-on-Hudson in New York, he prepared the thirteenth issue, a special tribute edition devoted to D. H. Lawrence that was published in the spring of 1926 in nearby Ossining, New York. Lawrence himself contributed poetry, prose, and a drawing of Pueblo Indian dancers, which accompanied art and writing by the friends he had made in New Mexico.

Johnson's decision to relocate *Laughing Horse* to the Southwest did not require changing the name of the publication. The founding editors had launched the magazine as "a merry horselaugh," which they stated in their inaugural edition.[8] In New Mexico, Johnson kept the name, having stumbled across a Navajo legend about a turquoise horse with a happy neigh, which perfectly suited a *Laughing Horse* stabled in the Southwest.

From Santa Fe to Taos

While living in Santa Fe, Johnson divided his time between working as Bynner's secretary and publishing *Laughing Horse*. Soon, however, Johnson's complex relationship with Bynner began to shift. Much has been written about Luhan's role in luring Johnson away from Santa Fe.

The biographers of Bynner and Johnson both report that Luhan was angry because she had been left out of the quartet of friends—Bynner, Johnson, D. H. Lawrence, and his wife, Frieda—who journeyed to Mexico in 1923. She wanted to exact revenge, so she hired Johnson to serve as her secretary in Taos. But other reasons affected the relationship between Johnson and Bynner. The two remained friends, but Johnson had grown tired of constantly being Bynner's student. Bynner's biographer, James Kraft, wrote that Johnson "was a quiet, subtle wit, slight and shy, and, finally, rather lazy about his talent. As he grew older he looked like a monk, and his single, quiet life became almost monastic. Bynner and he were lovers, but Spud was too indecisive to satisfy Bynner for long—he didn't respond to Bynner's teaching with alacrity."[9] Thus the time seemed right for Johnson to move to Taos. "But the separation was a gradual one, over several years. Though he spent much time in Taos beginning in 1924, it was not until 1927 that Johnson was actually installed as Mabel's secretary at Los Gallos."[10] There, with his foot-powered Kelsey printing press, Johnson continued to sporadically publish issues of *Laughing Horse* until 1939.

During the Depression, for example, *Laughing Horse* took a seven-year hiatus after the nineteenth issue came out in 1931. Not until 1938, with the discovery of new material, did Johnson publish the twentieth issue. Readers discovered that the wait had been worth it, for they received part of a satirical play, *Altitude*, written more than a decade earlier in Taos by D. H. Lawrence, who had died in 1930. The unfinished one-act play made fun of the pretensions of Luhan and Mary Austin as worshipers of Native American culture. Lawrence had set his play in Luhan's Taos house and even included Johnson in his satire.

Over the years, *Laughing Horse* examined an array of subjects. The seventeenth issue, for instance—a 1930 special edition on censorship—attacked legislation introduced in the U.S. Senate that attempted to censor imported books. "This meant, among other things, that D. H. Lawrence's new novel *Lady Chatterley's Lover* would be prohibited from entering the United States."[11] Having already experienced censorship firsthand, Johnson eagerly began a battle, soliciting contributions from New Mexico authors Bynner, Luhan, and Mary Austin as well as from poet Carl Sandburg, novelist Sherwood Anderson, social reformer Upton Sinclair, and Maxwell Perkins, then editor of *Scribner's Magazine*. Johnson also convinced U.S. Senator Bronson Cutting, who represented New Mexico, to oppose the legislation, and sent copies of the issue to every member of the U.S. Senate, which went on to defeat the legislation.

In 1939, Johnson published the twenty-first and final edition of his magazine with no announcement of its demise, which seemed in keeping with his subdued personality. During its lifetime, *Laughing Horse* played a unique role as one of America's small, avant-garde magazines. Its initial goal was to prod Americans out of their willingness to accept middle-class conventions and to make them question outdated beliefs they took for granted. After landing in the Southwest, it focused on examining and celebrating the art and culture of the region while frequently veering into the politics of censorship, Native American rights, and other subjects. Thus it reflected the trajectory of Johnson's own life as he moved from Berkeley to the Southwest and became enmeshed in the writers' colonies in Santa Fe and Taos. *Laughing Horse*'s quick-witted humor represented the personality of the man who single-handedly kept the little magazine in print as writer, editor, printer, and even advertising representative.

The Poet of *Laughing Horse*

While busy with *Laughing Horse* and working as Bynner's secretary, Johnson found time to write poetry and, with Bynner's advice, to submit it for publication. Soon his poetry and articles appeared in anthologies and literary journals. While he did publish his own writing in *Laughing Horse*, his work also ran in *Poetry, New Republic,* and other national magazines that did not carry his name on the masthead.

Johnson had access to advice from the experts. Bynner critiqued his work, as did D. H. Lawrence during the months he spent in Taos in 1924 and 1925, employing Johnson as his secretary. Johnson was so independent, however, that he could not remain a student to anyone for long. "Spud refused to commit himself to anyone," wrote Bynner's biographer James Kraft.[12]

By 1926, Johnson's reputation as a poet earned him an invitation to write an essay about poetry in the Southwest for the *Anthology of Magazine Verse and Yearbook of American Poetry*. The resulting piece conveyed "a sensitivity to the multicultural literary sources of modern southwestern poetry, including Spanish and Mexican songs, cowboy ballads, and Indian poetry," Udall wrote. "He gives credit to the pervasive influence of Bynner and Austin, but he recognizes the promise of emerging poets as well."[13]

Johnson considered himself one of those emerging poets. When he joined Writers' Editions, a cooperative publishing group organized by a handful of Santa Fe writers in the mid-1930s, readers had a chance to see what an accomplished poet he was. Each author participating in the venture paid to have his or her work published and then received 90 percent of the profits from the sale of their books. *Horizontal Yellow*, published in 1935, contained fifty-six poems by Johnson, a mixture of new works and others previously published in magazines and anthologies.

Horizontal Yellow contained the proof that Johnson was a skilled poet who could write sparingly, yet eloquently, about numerous topics, from Pueblo culture to the difficulties of aging. The final lines of "Taos Dance," for example, lyrically reveal the poet's experience witnessing a ceremonial dance at Taos Pueblo:

> Thundersticks and eagle bones
> Voices, gestures, and the drums,
> Merged into a single rhythm,
> The living heart-beat of the drum.

Taos House

In Taos, Johnson moved into a small adobe house with just a few rooms, where he lived until his death in 1968. Located at a bend in the road now called Paseo del Pueblo Norte, the house still stands and is today a funky bed and breakfast fittingly named The Laughing Horse Inn, though it has changed greatly since Johnson's heyday. Yet the original rooms occupied by Johnson still exist, including the bathroom he transformed into a morning room, creating a couch by placing a board covered with a Native American blanket across the tub. He also added a room, built around a covered well that became his coffee table, where he placed plants and flowers. The room was filled with books, magazines, and his beloved press—all attesting to Johnson's love of the printed word. From this small adobe, Johnson printed new issues of *Laughing Horse* and wrote columns that appeared in the *New Yorker* as well as numerous other publications.

Johnson befriended many of the notables who visited the region, including artist Georgia O'Keeffe. Johnson and O'Keeffe met in Taos when O'Keeffe spent her first summer in New Mexico in 1929 as a guest of Mabel's. The two struck up a long-lasting friendship that summer, embarking on a driving tour of the West with a few other friends. They evidently enjoyed each other's company because they took another road trip together in October 1934, when Johnson drove her back to New York City in her Ford after O'Keeffe had spent yet another summer in New Mexico. Tension arose at least once during the long drive: when O'Keeffe griped about their lodgings and breakfast, Johnson recorded in his journal that she was "more persnickety and old-maidish than usual."[14] Like good friends who can weather disagreements, however, Johnson and O'Keeffe kept up their friendship after O'Keeffe had settled in Abiquiu in 1949. Udall described the attraction: "To O'Keeffe and to many other women, Johnson was a non-threatening friend, in part because of his homosexuality. Besides, they liked him for his vital interest in life and literature, and for his astute, often wry, observations on human nature."[15]

Johnson's witticisms appealed to many others as well. While visiting Mabel Dodge Luhan in Croton-on-Hudson, New York, during the winter of 1925–26, he contributed pieces to the *New Yorker*, which debuted on February 21, 1925. The editors liked his work so much they asked him to become a regular contributor to the magazine. "Johnson's *New Yorker* sketches are breezy, irreverent, and youthful—writing aimed at a socially ambitious, jazz-age readership," Udall wrote.[16]

Johnson was the one writer of this era who felt as comfortable in Taos as he did in Santa Fe. In turn, the writing communities in both places accepted him. He wrote a popular gossip column, "The Perambulator," and a literary column for the *Santa Fe New Mexican* in 1930 and served as editor of the *Taos Valley News* from 1933 to 1935. He also managed the popular Villagra Bookshop, owned by Roberta Robey, in Santa Fe's Sena Plaza.

In 1938, Johnson launched *The Horse Fly*, a one-sheet weekly newspaper filled with all the news he considered fit to print. The miniature paper "chronicled the comings and goings of residents, promoted arts events, and proclaimed causes dear to its editor's heart," Udall wrote, adding that the one-man operation "was a labor of love."[17]

Johnson labored for one year exactly, as a reporter, advertiser, typesetter, and distributor of fifty-two issues before fatigue forced him to fold *The Horse Fly*.

"As a newspaper columnist, he served as the gentle crusader, the mildly buzzing, persistent gadfly,"[18] wrote his friend Claire Morrill, who co-owned the popular, longstanding Taos Book Shop, where Johnson briefly worked cataloging out-of-print books. His figure was familiar around Taos, whether wearing a deer-stalker's cap or a wig when age began to thin out his hair, as Morrill reported, adding, "A professional bachelor, he was the only gregarious hermit I ever knew, and the only man, who, in a roomful of people, could sit silently in a corner all evening smoking his Sherlock Holmes pipe, and still often manage to give the impression of having taken a pleasant and active part in the proceedings."[19]

As the colonies began to wane, Johnson kept up a freelance career. In his later years, he took on such controversial topics as development, the environment, and racism in "The Santa Fe Gadfly," his Sunday column that appeared in the *Santa Fe New Mexican* more than three hundred times before he died in 1968. His opinions mattered to his neighbors and friends. He was "the aesthetic and intellectual conscience of Taos," Morrill wrote. "He warned when meretricious elements crept in with change; he was the watchdog of intellectual integrity and the voice of reason raised against ideological extremes."[20] As devoted as he was to the solitary writer's life, Johnson took part in the community as a participant in theater events and annual parades. During the years of World War II, he sold books from a portable cart close to the Taos plaza to supplement his income.

Johnson also developed a serious interest in art. He studied drawing in Taos art classes, producing simple pen-and-ink works that conveyed a reverence for the places and people that mattered to him. Johnson put his artist's eye to work during a 1960 rafting trip along the Colorado River with a group of friends that included Morrill and photographer Eliot Porter. The journey yielded *Six Taoseños Who Braved the Colorado River*, a small book of Johnson's drawings, Porter's photographs, and text by Johnson and Merrill.

As the 1960s progressed, Johnson's health declined. He was helping friends assemble a Taos exhibit of his drawings when he died in

Willard "Spud" Johnson, date unknown. Courtesy Harwood
Museum of Art of the University of New Mexico. No. 1445.86.

November 1968, just a few months after Bynner. The show opened as a memorial, where his "sensitive drawings were the big attraction, with most selling for a mere five dollars or so."[21]

The poet and founder of *Laughing Horse* "was a man whose life and art were never separated," Udall wrote.[22] A visit to his former home reveals the aptness of this observation. It is easy to imagine Johnson, pipe firmly planted in mouth, relaxing in the room where he once kept his Kelsey printing press and his beloved collection of books, editing copy for *Laughing Horse* or composing a poem about the town that became his home for more than four decades.

Spud Johnson had "an elfin grace and a modulated voice," according to John Collier Jr., who recalled his childhood memories of Johnson in his foreword to the 1987 edition of Mabel Dodge Luhan's *Edge of Taos Desert*.[23] That grace and voice reached far and wide through *Laughing Horse,* as well as the poetry and articles Johnson wrote from his small Taos house, celebrating the beauty and complexity of the region for the world to read.

CHAPTER ELEVEN

Frank Waters

FRANK WATERS ARRIVED in Taos in 1937 as the literary colonies were starting to wane. Yet his twenty-seven books of fiction and nonfiction, particularly the ones about Native Americans, extended to new levels the deep mysteries of New Mexico that had fascinated Mabel Dodge Luhan, Mary Austin, Witter Bynner, and other members of the Santa Fe and Taos colonies.

Early Awareness

Waters claimed to be part Native American himself. He was born in 1902 at the foot of Pike's Peak in Colorado Springs, Colorado, to a father Waters later described as one-quarter Cheyenne and a mother whose Southern family had moved West in the late 1800s. Like Mary Austin, he had an early childhood experience that opened his mind and heart to a world beyond the ordinary. After gold had been discovered on Pike's Peak in 1891, his maternal grandfather, a successful building contractor, joined the fevered rush to find more of the precious metal, opening his own Colorado mines. While the young Waters was playing with sand at one of his grandfather's Cripple Creek mines, he noticed the uniqueness of every grain and, "in an instant, Pike's Peak took on a different meaning," he wrote in his memoir. "I saw

Frank Waters, date unknown. Courtesy the Harwood Museum of Art of the
University of New Mexico. No. 168.81.

that it was composed of all these millions of grains of sand, which were mysteriously and precisely fitted together into one mighty, single whole—a sacred place of power, as the Utes regarded it."[1] This was the first of many mystical experiences that marked his life and consequently infused his writing, which focused on such an enormous range of human experience that critics have found it difficult to summarize. Perhaps Albuquerque author Rudolfo Anaya put it best, writing in his foreword to Frank Waters's memoir *Of Time and Change* that Waters consistently wrote about "the interconnectedness of life on Earth and throughout the universe . . . In his novels and in his non-fiction books, he provided us glimpses into that Otherworld he sought."[2]

When Waters was twelve, his father died, but not before he had introduced his son to Native American culture during visits to a Navajo trading post. There Waters learned that like the Utes, the Navajos "regarded the land as their Mother Earth," lessons that left a deep impression upon the boy.[3]

Waters studied engineering at Colorado College, then dropped out in his third year and took off to see the world. He took a job laying pipes in Wyoming's Salt Creek oil field and then another working as a telephone engineer with the Southern California Telephone Company, which sent him to Olympia Valley, situated on the border of California and Mexico's Baja California. Experiencing the California desert inspired Waters to write his first novel, *Fever Pitch*, published in 1930. The book was "an instant flop," as Waters acknowledged, but that didn't deter him.[4] When the phone company transferred him to a desk job in Los Angeles, he grew impatient, quit, and lit out to become a full-time writer, traveling the Southwest for years, writing "anything that could be sold."[5]

Finding the Spirit of Taos

Waters journeyed across the Southwest like a nomad, living in numerous places. In 1937, he traveled to Taos for the first time and rented Spud Johnson's house. While attending a Native American dance, he met Luhan's husband, Tony, who invited Waters to attend a party at Luhan's Los Gallos estate. Waters accepted, and during the party he found Luhan to be "friendly and warm and it destroyed my bad impressions of her immediately," he told Luhan's biographer, Lois Palken Rudnick. "I liked her very much."[6]

Waters felt the same way about Taos. He took up residence in several places, including an old hotel in Mora, southeast of Taos, and in a house Luhan owned in Placita, next door to where Spud Johnson finally bought a house. He stayed there even after novelist Myron Brinig bought the house, helping the writer to make repairs and fix up the house so he could live there comfortably. In 1947, Waters bought his own adobe house in Arroyo Seco, a tiny town outside of Taos. Living at an elevation of 8,600 feet on a slope of the Sangre de Cristo Mountains, surrounded by aspen and cottonwood trees, Waters thrived on his intimacy with the natural world, in which he found profound signs of a mysterious, creative force.

The Taos region appealed to Waters as one of the most beautiful places in the world, "imbued with a curious charisma, an indefinable attraction, a compulsive magnetism."[7] He suggested in his memoir that the potency of the place might be due to the solemn presence of Taos Pueblo's Sacred Mountain, which he believed possessed a "timeless spirit."[8]

Waters tapped deeply into the spirit he felt in Taos. He was in the town courthouse the day that a Taos Pueblo man, Frank Samora, was found guilty and fined for slaying a deer out of season in the Carson National Forest. This incident took root in his imagination and, just a few days later, as he stood in his bathroom shaving, the sink basin became a sort of magical scrying bowl offering a vision of three men:

the regional Spanish head of the Forest service, the blanketed Indian governor of Taos Pueblo, and an Anglo man whom I couldn't quite identify. They appeared to be arguing over the judgment upon the guilty Indian who had killed the deer in the mountains.[9]

Waters found himself staring at the inspiration for *The Man Who Killed the Deer*, his fictionalized account of Samora's plight that was published in 1942. From the moment Waters began to write the novel, "it unfolded like a flower in its own inherent pattern" and the book remains a classic today.[10] The story focuses on Martiniano, a young man from the fictional La Oreja Pueblo who must discover his true self while navigating life in the traditional Pueblo world and in the encroaching white world. The living Pueblo culture that Waters witnessed in Taos relied on ancient traditions and beliefs tied to nature for order and harmony, and this became a major theme in *The Man Who Killed the Deer*. In the novel, Waters described his firm belief in "the simple and monstrous truth of mankind's solidarity with all that breathes and does not breathe, all that has lived and shall live again upon the unfathomed breast of the earth we trod so lightly, beneath the stars that glimmer less brightly but more enduringly than our own brief lives."[11]

Native American scholar Vine Deloria wrote that the "breadth" Waters displayed in his writing "discourages any ordinary mortal from picking a theme and proclaiming it definitive."[12] Waters indeed covered an astonishing number of topics—from the experiences of Colorado miners to traditional Hispano family life, the religion and mythology of the Hopi, the deep, civilization-changing implications of the atomic bomb, and more. Yet one continuous thread ran through his work: "the belief that a great force of spirit connected all living things, a force that would transform our consciousness by merging the 'rational with the intuitive,'" as his biographer John Nizalowski wrote in an introduction to an anthology of essays commemorating the centennial of the birth of Waters.[13]

Waters possessed a lifelong interest in the mythology, spirituality, and life cycles of the Native Americans, including the highly guarded Hopi people, whom he spent two years living with before he wrote his 1963 nonfiction work *The Book of the Hopi*. For Deloria, the book contained "the most comprehensive presentation of Hopi traditions."[14] The warm, easygoing manner Waters projected, even with strangers, coupled with his serious interest in other cultures, earned him the trust of the Hopi, who typically do not share any aspect of their cultural or spiritual practices with outsiders.

At Otowi Crossing with Peggy Pond Church

Waters merged his deep respect for the mystical aspects of life with an avid interest in science. From 1953 to 1956, he worked as an information specialist for the Atomic Energy Commission at the Los Alamos Scientific Laboratory. He may even have worked for the government on a covert mission in Santa Fe to seek out German or Russian spies sniffing around for information about the atomic bomb being invented at the nearby lab. During these years, he lived on Jacona Road in Pojoaque, near the place where Edith Warner (1893–1951) spent the last twenty years of her life. Warner, the shy daughter of a Baptist minister from Pennsylvania, came to New Mexico to recover from illness and ended up with the odd job of working as a freight agent for a narrow-gauge railroad line by the Rio Grande at the Otowi Switch. Initially she lived in a small, rustic house and later built a new residence. When the railroad line was shut down, Warner opened a legendary tearoom that became a popular gathering spot for many of the scientists working at Los Alamos, who shared lively discussions while eating simple, hearty dinners prepared by Warner, followed by her famous chocolate cake. Considered by many to be a mystic of sorts herself, Warner was the subject of Peggy Pond Church's classic 1959 nonfiction book *The House at Otowi Bridge*, which explored Warner's close connection to nearby San Ildefonso Pueblo and the surrounding land she grew to love, both of which shaped her strong sense of spirituality.

Born in 1903 in Watrous, New Mexico, Church was an acclaimed Southwest poet who served as a founding member of Writers' Editions and wrote eight books of verse and a biography of Mary Austin, published after Austin died. *Poetry* and the *Saturday Review of Literature* regularly published Church's work. She grew up on the Pajarito Plateau, where her father founded the Los Alamos Ranch School in 1917 as a small and elite boy's prep school with a maximum of forty-eight students aged twelve to eighteen. The staff devoted itself to combining a top-notch academic program with outdoor wilderness skills. At least two of its students achieved international literary fame—Gore Vidal and William S. Burroughs. When the U.S. government decided to open its top-secret bomb production facility in Los Alamos, it forced the school to close in 1943. Church and her family had to leave their beloved plateau, yet Church could not abandon New Mexico. Except for her studies at Smith College and the three years she spent in Berkeley, California, Church lived her life among New Mexico's mountains and mesas. She died in Santa Fe at age eighty-two in 1986. (As a side note, her younger brother Ashley Pond became a physician who treated Mabel Dodge Luhan in a Taos hospital that Luhan provided funding to help build.)

Church grew to admire Warner and became her friend. In *House at Otowi Bridge*, she merged their lives, writing about the disinheritance of her own family's land while poetically extolling Warner's New Mexico experience. Her book offers strong evidence that Church would have enjoyed a life like Warner's and perhaps could have, had the U.S. government not taken over Pajarito Plateau. Church's *House at Otowi Bridge* offers a poignant look at how Warner forged a spiritual relationship with the land and people of New Mexico and friendships with Los Alamos scientists Robert Oppenheimer, Neils Bohr, and others. Church's book also describes Warner's friendship with Tilano, an older San Ildefonso Pueblo man who eventually moved in with her.

In 2001, Texas Tech University Press published *Bones Incandescent: The Pajarito Journals of Peggy Pond Church*, with more than fifty journals Church wrote between the 1930s and 1986. Her writings chronicle the intimate relationship she forged with the natural world of her childhood as well as with other women writers of the Southwest who wrote about a sense of place, including Edith Warner, Mary Austin, and May Sarton, according to the book's editor, American studies scholar Shelly Armitage, who also wrote contributing essays. *Accidental Magic*, a posthumous collection published in 2004 by Wildflower Press, contains more than five hundred unpublished works found in file drawers and letters placed in Church's journals. Kathleen Church, the author's daughter-in-law, wrote the foreword.

Living so close to Warner's residence and tearoom must have inspired Waters to write his 1966 novel *Woman at Otowi Crossing*. As explained by Patrick Burns, who edited and annotated the University of New Mexico Press's 2001 anthology *In the Shadow of Los Alamos: Selected Writings of Edith Warner*, Waters loosely based his protagonist, Helen Chalmers, on Edith Warner, but the liberties he took with his fictional story upset loyal fans of Church's book. Chalmers, for example, was divorced and abandoned her daughter, yet Warner neither married nor had children. Chalmers also had an affair with an Anglo man, though Warner's relationship with Tilano remains unclear. Supporters of Waters's novel believed that Church had written a book better described as autobiography than biography because she included so much information about her own life. Waters responded to his detractors by stating that he based his novel not on history but on the myth that evolved about the sage and solitary woman who died of cancer in 1951.[15] "Like all legends, the story of Edith Warner's life changes with the storytellers," Burns wrote.[16] Indeed, both books endure, and Waters and Church amiably agreed not to disagree years ago, though some readers still debate which book contains more truth.

A Mystic in Taos

Waters has been called America's greatest unknown writer. Even though he was nominated several times for a Nobel Prize in literature, his books remain relatively unknown. But then perhaps the search for meaning and enlightenment mattered more to this writer than achieving international literary fame. Waters died in 1995 at age ninety-two in his Arroyo Seco home, leaving behind a cult of readers. His ashes are buried beneath an aspen tree on his property. His books continue to attract new fans, including those who believe that his books can help lift an ailing civilization into an enlightened realm. As Nizalowski wrote, "the words of Frank Waters will be an important catalyst for humanity's transformation."[17] The Frank Waters Foundation, established at his Arroyo Seco home in 1993 before his death and now overseen by Barbara Waters, his widow, devotes itself to furthering the author's interests by "sheltering the creative spirit" through residencies offered to writers, photographers, and musicians.

Waters traveled often, but in northern New Mexico he connected with the spirit of the land and its indigenous people to discover a truth that resonates throughout his work: "One of the greatest lessons I finally learned is that this source in which everything is interconnected into one harmonious whole—the nebulous Otherworld I had imagined so long ago—does not exist somewhere among the splendor of the midnight stars, but within ourselves."[18]

PART THREE

A Memorable
Literary Landscape

CHAPTER TWELVE

Significant Others

SOME OF THE WRITERS connected with the Santa Fe and Taos literary colonies held less prominent positions than Mabel Dodge Luhan, Alice Corbin Henderson, and other authors included thus far in this book. Other authors who wrote about northern New Mexico established their reputations outside of the state. A few have simply faded from memory along with their books. This chapter briefly explores the lives and work of five such authors who contributed important books during the colony era. Many of their books are now out of print but are worth seeking out in libraries and used bookstores for their valuable viewpoints about life in New Mexico.

Lynn Riggs: The Father of the Folk Play

American playwright, screenwriter, poet, and Guggenheim fellow Rollie Lynn Riggs (1899–1954) stepped off the train in Lamy one bright fall day in 1923. He had just left behind his life as a promising student attending the University of Oklahoma, his native state. Bynner, who had been a visiting lecturer at the school during the previous winter, met Riggs when the student seemed to be struggling with consumption, depression, a nervous breakdown, or some other ailment difficult to diagnose. Concerned, Bynner urged him to travel to Santa Fe's Sunmount Sanatorium as a restorative pilgrimage.

Riggs left school "in the midst of his senior year, the place of his greatest happiness, his many successes and honors, and had left there everything he cared about," wrote his biographer Phyllis Cole Braunlich. "None of it was recoverable: the teaching assistantship, the life of a promising student-poet, the fraternity, the almost-won bachelor's degree, and the beauty queen with raven hair and violet eyes who had slipped out of his arms and eloped with someone else."[1]

Riggs hoped Sunmount's healthy diet, dry desert air, and brilliant sunlight would cure him the same way it cured Bynner and Henderson before him. For the past twenty years, countless other patients had checked into the famous facility for rest and recuperation within the rooms of the two-story main lodge and its tent-topped square cottages dotting the hillside, surrounded by aspen and cottonwood trees and a golden lawn. Within a few months, Riggs joined the ranks of the healthy. On December 3 of that year, he wrote Bynner, who then was in New York, "Feeling much better, thanks to you. Only it will take several decades to overcome wrong habits of thought, won't it? I'm beginning Decade 1 . . . I finished a thing called 'Sanatorium' [*sic*] . . . and am two scenes deep in a one-act play; hope to finish 'Santa Fe' right away . . . Hal, you saved my life, you know—to Humanity the burden."[2]

Riggs may actually have been recovering from a difficult childhood while at Sunmount. Braunlich wrote,

> Santa Fe's free acceptance buoyed his spirit, stifled from a youth spent in a home filled with rejection and criticism. Santa Fe in its long history of invasions had learned tolerance; first were the Indians, then came the Spanish explorers, then Hispanic and American pioneers and businessmen, then archaeologists, vacationers, and health-seekers. Taking them all in stride, local businessmen mingled freely with the writers and artists and held celebrity dinner parties which helped the humble adobe poets stay alive.[3]

Riggs described the Sunmount scene himself in a November 1923 letter to one of his former professors:

"Sunmount," where I am staying, is full of tubercular patients from everywhere: there is a Miss Conkey next to me who lives in New York and reads a lot, and is a friend of all the wild young radicals who come out of Chicago and Denver—Ivor Winters, Janet Lewis, John Meem, etc.; there is a Mlle. Breviere, who has a sun-bath every morning—her legs are a rich chocolate with overtones of smoldering red like an overheated stove; there is a Katherine Stinson, a famous flyer, who was in the A.E.F. in France and is now down with T.B.—she's a Texas girl; . . . there is a young Harvard graduate who likes Havelock Ellis, and damns the "young genera-tion"—as I do . . . Tell everybody I'm alive.[4]

Riggs's biographer imagined that his arrival in Santa Fe may have had something to do with the end of the state's three-year drought as well as the discovery of oil on the Navajo Reserve, both of which took place during Riggs's first year in town. If she guessed correctly, then Santa Fe delivered a few gifts in return to Riggs. He starting writing poems almost as soon he arrived that were published in *Laughing Horse*, including his most famous poem, "Morning Walk—Santa Fe." Other Santa Fe poems appeared in *New Republic* and *American Mercury*. *Laughing Horse*'s ninth issue, published in December 1923, contained Riggs's poem "Sanatarium"—which describes "a woman with hair the color of corn shucks in a tuberculosis sanatarium."[5]

Corn shucks appear at least a few times in the writings by this Oklahoman native, who was born on August 31, 1899, in Claremore, Oklahoma. His mother, who was part Cherokee, died shortly after his birth from typhoid fever, and his life seemed marked by "a unique sense of beauty and his personal anguish."[6] Once he discovered his voice in Santa Fe, Riggs's plays received heaps of critical acclaim. He wrote twenty-one full-length plays as well as one-act and television plays, short stories, and poetry. He also led the "little theater" move-ment of the 1930s. His plays "used the authentic colloquial speech of early Oklahoma,"[7] which sings out in his greatest legacy, *Green Grow the Lilacs*. This Broadway hit debuted in 1931, before Rogers and Hammerstein used it as the basis for their musical classic *Oklahoma!*, which debuted in 1943.

Like Spud Johnson, Riggs worked briefly as a secretary to Bynner, with whom he had an affair. He developed other close ties to the town, especially with the formidable actress and sculptor Ida Rauh Eastman, who moved to Santa Fe from New York in 1922 with her young son after divorcing her husband, political writer Max Eastman. A leader of the popular Provincetown Players on Cape Cod, she directed the first one-act play by Eugene O'Neill, *Where the Cross Is Made*. Women's rights activist Margaret Sanger greatly influenced her. While distributing pamphlets advocating birth control in 1916 at age thirty-six, she was arrested and charged with obscenity. Her freedom of spirit impressed Riggs. She "did more than anyone to put Lynn Riggs back on the track of his career, and she was his friend both in need and in good times the rest of his life."[8]

Riggs's reputation remains intact as one of the more creative and experimental writers of the Depression era. Although he later divided his time between Hollywood, New York, and Chapel Hill, Santa Fe marks the place where he made the fortuitous decision to devote his life to writing plays.

Raymond Otis: Early Writer of the Golden Era

Raymond Otis visited Santa Fe as a child and then returned in 1927 to live and work as a writer. Born in Chicago in 1900, he graduated from Yale in 1924 and wrote "seven novels, two of which were published in England and one in America, many short stories, two plays and one article," as he outlined in a February 24, 1937, letter answering an accusation that because he was wealthy, he should not be employed by the New Mexico Federal Writers' Project (NMFWP).[9] He itemized his debts and explained that he was a hardworking, "property-poor" writer. His tack worked because poet, journalist, and lecturer Ina Sizer Cassidy, wife of Santa Fe painter Gerald Cassidy, earned him the right to keep his job. Cassidy secured her job as NMFWP's state director after John Collier had recommended her appointment. She held the group's initial meetings in her Canyon Road home. Cassidy had numerous reporting, editing, translating, coordinating projects to oversee, but soon, severely disgruntled factions of her group focused their complaints on her. Poet Norman Macleod spent the summer of 1936 working for the NMFWP. In his 1939 autobiographical novel *You Get What You Ask For*, he wrote candidly about his Santa Fe experience: "that redoubtable elderly woman . . . Mrs. Crotchety [Cassidy]—whose only claim

Raymond Otis, 1934. Courtesy Nathaniel Owings.

to being literary resided in the fact that she had written several rather sketchy poems about lover come back to me, etc., and her assistant, Mrs. Alice Hendricks [Henderson], yes-woman . . . and a poet—a rather good one, in fact." Macleod went on to describe why the novel's protagonist quits Santa Fe:

> . . . where the beer cost so much . . . There was nothing for him in Santa Fe, that entr'acte for escapists. Mecca for tuberculars, where death splintered wooden coffins into the crucifixes of defeat! The life of Santa Fe was buried in the past. The Trojan women on the Federal Writers' Project in New Mexico could have their astrology! D. H. Lawrence had said—the light blinds them. There was too much sunlight and they couldn't get out of the darkness.[10]

Otis undoubtedly enjoyed Santa Fe more than MacLeod but he, too, wrote a book portraying Santa Fe in thinly disguised fiction before an early death in 1938 from nephritis. His 1934 roman à clef, *Fire in the Night*, is not easy to find but worth digging for as it offers an insider's view of Santa Fe life during 1931, when the writers' colony was heating up. The saga unfolds during a series of deliberately set fires to reveal adultery, alcoholism, and other troubles that plague a small town populated by longtime Hispano families and recently arrived Anglo artists and authors. One of the main characters, a domineering writer known as The Princess, strongly resembles Mary Austin. Not surprisingly, Otis was a member of Santa Fe's Volunteer Fire Company. He also wrote the 1936 coming-of-age-novel *Miguel of the Bright Mountain* and the 1937 novel *Little Valley* and was a founding member of the cooperative publishing venture Writers' Editions. In "The Santa Fe Group," a December 8, 1934, article in *Saturday Review of Literature* written by Elizabeth Shepley Sergeant, she described Otis: "He has some of the characteristics of the woodland creature—even to faun ears, and eyes set a little crooked in his head,—he will bear watching."[11] Today, his books still bear reading.

Haniel Long: Poet of Distinction

Haniel Long, born in 1888 in Burma where his parents were Methodist missionaries, settled in Santa Fe in 1929. Although his reputation as an original, intuitive poet of several acclaimed books has languished over the years, his work reveals a sensitive insight into human nature and other cultures.

Long's Santa Fe connection took root through the complicated friendship he forged with Witter Bynner, whom he met in 1908 while studying at Harvard. According to Bynner's biographer James Kraft, the two

Haniel Long, date unknown. Courtesy Palace
of the Governors (MNM/DCA). Neg. no. 158457.

bonded over American literature in a relationship that cast Bynner as the father figure and mentor. Kraft wrote that the two became lovers in the beginning of their friendship, "and perhaps at various times thereafter," forming one of the oldest, most challenging relationships of Bynner's life.[12] Long's desire to develop his own literary voice and his marriage in 1913 to a learned and well-traveled woman, who was overweight and spoke in a high-pitched voice, posed the biggest problems for Bynner. "The real point seems to be that in marrying her, Long had rejected Bynner, as Long would over the years reject Bynner's artistic influence and go in a direction decidedly different from Bynner's."[13]

Long started teaching English at the Carnegie Institute of Technology in Pittsburgh in 1910 and in 1920 became the head of the English Department. He visited Bynner in Santa Fe several times during the 1920s. Then, suffering a breakdown, he moved with his wife to Santa Fe in 1929 to recover and pursue a writing career. He became active in the Santa Fe writers' colony as a founding member of Writers' Editions and a participant in the Poets' Roundups. He also signed on as editor of "The New Mexico Writers' Page," a literary section launched in the weekly Albuquerque newspaper *New Mexico Sentinel* in 1937 and billed as "a weekly page of prose and verse contributed by New Mexicans, at home or abroad."[14] The paper's editor moved the *Sentinel* to Santa Fe, where Long continued to edit what became known simply as the "Writers' Page," filled with his own writings as well as contributions from the page's associates—Witter Bynner, Paul Horgan, Frieda Lawrence, and Erna Fergusson—and other writers, including Peggy Pond Church. When the page folded in 1939, Long penned a farewell column in which he lauded the literary energy in Santa Fe: "Here in New Mexico we are living on a volcano of expressiveness, and the lid may blow off any day." He added that "every third New Mexican wrote verses, every fourth had a novel concealed in his desk and every fifth was just finishing a four-act play."[15]

Long's own literary contributions have been severely overlooked. Writers' Editions published two of his poetry collections—*Atlantides* in 1933 and *Pittsburgh Memoranda* in 1935. His innovative 1936 novella *Interlinear to Cabeza de Vaca* offers an imaginative and progressive view of the sixteenth-century Spanish explorer's experiences with "savages" he encountered on the North American continent. The book, which explores the innate goodness that can motivate humans, impressed Henry Miller to write an introduction to a British edition and also moved poet and novelist May Sarton to extol it in her 1976 book *A World of Light: Portraits and Celebrations*, after visiting her friend Long in Santa Fe in December 1940.

Long's friendship with Bynner broke off in 1948 during a dinner party when Bynner's longtime companion, Robert Hunt, became drunk and made insulting remarks about Jewish people, so outraging the Longs that they cut all ties. "This incident was the single most disturbing social experience of Bynner's life," Kraft wrote. "It hung in his mind like some dead carcass and he returned to it again and again, but he was unable to get rid of it."[16] Bynner and Long had a "superficial reconciliation" at Bynner's seventy-fifth birthday party in 1956. Two months later, Long died on October 17 at the Mayo Clinic in Minnesota and his wife died three days after that in Santa Fe.[17] Bynner read from Long's poetry at the couple's joint funeral.

The following fragment from Long's sketch "Cerrillos Hills" reveals the poet's love for New Mexico's landscape: "Those cones of turquoise to the southwest draw my thoughts like a magnet. They never reveal themselves; the more I gaze at them the more they clothe themselves in their mysterious garments."[18]

Erna and Harvey Fergusson: Celebrating New Mexico Cultures

Two years separated Erna Fergusson from her younger brother Harvey, both of whom were born and raised in Albuquerque. They shared an impressive ability to write about the Southwest with conviction, which linked them to the literary colonies in Santa Fe and Taos. Because Erna traveled widely but spent most of her life in Albuquerque, she had more contact with the colonies than Harvey, who never again lived permanently in the Southwest after graduating from Washington and Lee University in Lexington, Virginia.

The Fergussons' maternal grandfather was a successful businessman in Albuquerque and their father, Harvey Butler Fergusson, served as New Mexico's first U.S. congressman after the territory became a state. Both Erna and Harvey worked as journalists before beginning their literary careers. Erna primarily wrote travel literature and Harvey became an acclaimed novelist who also wrote nonfiction and screenplays for Hollywood.

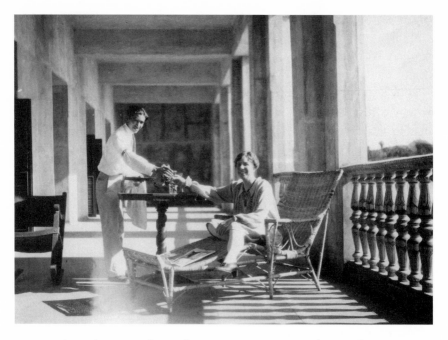

Erna Fergusson, date unknown. Courtesy Center for Southwest
Research, University Libraries, University of New Mexico.
No. 000–045–0002 from the Erna Fergusson Collection.

Erna's stint as field director for the Red Cross in New Mexico during World War I took her into New Mexico's small towns and villages,
where she gained a deep respect for multicultural aspects of the state.
This appreciation for New Mexico led her to launch Koshare Tours
with the help of her friend Ethel Hickey in 1921. The highly successful business venture catered to tourists, offering them a chance to see
the "Indian country" of New Mexico, Southern Colorado, and Arizona.
Guests visited natural landmarks, attended Native American dances,
and slept under the stars if no Pueblo home, hotel, or ranch was available. Koshare Tours took its name from "the Pueblo dancers who, as
emissaries of the gods, were called the 'delight makers' by [Adolph]
Bandelier," the discoverer of the Native American ruins that now bear
his name—Bandelier National Monument near Santa Fe.[19]

Indeed, Erna and her friend designed the tours to impart delight.

Clients traveled by motor car for up to several days, accompanied by female guides dressed in tailored tan suits, velvet Navajo blouses, slimmed-down Stetson hats, and Native American jewelry. Erna, often joined by Santa Fe poet Alice Corbin Henderson, trained the guides to be able to lecture for hours about the region's history and culture. Lunch and afternoon tea were part of the deal, too, along with a muscled man who could help out in case the car broke down, became mired in mud, or encountered some other kind of emergency. The tours became so popular that Fred Harvey, founder of the famed Harvey House hotels, merged Koshare Tours into his own Harvey Indian Detours in 1926.

The success of Koshare Tours proved to Erna that the Southwest held a great deal of interest to people around the country. Inspired, she wrote her first book, *Dancing Gods*, published in 1931 and considered by Southwestern literature authority Lawrence Clark Powell to be her finest book. Powell praised *Dancing Gods* as "the best of all books about the Indian ceremonials of New Mexico and Arizona."[20] Powell particularly admired Erna's decision not to explain the Native Americans, but to describe their cultural differences, explaining that Anglos, for instance, use song and dance chiefly as entertainment, while Native Americans rely on song and dance to bring rain, a plentiful harvest, and a successful hunt—or, in other words, life.[21]

Dancing Gods sold so well that its publisher, Alfred A. Knopf, handled most of her subsequent books. Erna began her relationship with Knopf, who also published her brother's books, after meeting him in Santa Fe at the home of Santa Fe poet Witter Bynner, another of Knopf's authors. She kept close ties to the writers' colonies in Santa Fe and Taos, having established friendships with Haniel Long, Paul Horgan, and Peggy Pond Church. Mabel Dodge Luhan hired her in the late 1920s to transform her Taos estate into a guesthouse for paying visitors, but the project never took place.

Erna wrote thirteen books and each combined travel with history, including volumes on New Mexico, Hawaii, Latin America, Mexican cooking, and a popular collection of true-life, spine-tingling tales, *Murder and Mystery in New Mexico*. Her 1951 book *New Mexico, a Pageant of Three Peoples* traces the histories of Anglo, Native American, and Spanish culture in her native state and became a classic. Her biographer Robert Franklin Gish noted that by merging her own impressions with a history she researched meticulously, she could bring a place to life, especially when she wrote about the place she knew the best—the Southwest: "All of Fergusson's Southwestern writings implicitly contain this assumption of the close relationship between travel and history, complemented by the belief that, in New Mexico especially, history is part of the living, immediate present, 'here, now . . . going on.'"[22]

Erna worked up until her death from cancer at age seventy-six in 1964. Her passion for her native landscape provided ample material for a life devoted to literature that continues to be read today.

Harvey shared his sister's interest in the Southwest, even though he left the region. He spent a decade in Washington, D.C., as a political reporter for numerous newspapers and met editor, author, and cofounder of *American Mercury* H. L. Mencken, who helped launch Harvey's career with his first novel, *The Blood of the Conquerors*, published by Knopf in 1921. The story hinges on Hispano and Anglo cultures vying for power in twentieth-century New Mexico and its modest success allowed Fergusson to quit his day job and become a freelance writer, a career he sustained until his death in Berkeley, California, in 1971 at age eighty-one.

Harvey moved to New York to begin screenwriting and then wrote three more novels, including *Hot Saturday*, which satirizes Albuquerque. Unhappy reactions from Albuquerque residents made clear to Harvey that his decision to live in New York was a wise one. He also made trips to Hollywood for his screenwriting work, which included a 1932 film version of *Hot Saturday* starring Cary Grant.

Powell considered Harvey's first four novels as "apprentice work" that paved the way for his "masterpiece of historical-poetical prose," *Wolf Song*, published in 1927, the same year Willa Cather's Southwestern classic *Death Comes for the Archbishop* was published.[23] *Wolf Song* eloquently pays tribute to the mountain men and beaver trappers who roamed the Sangre de Cristo Mountains during the nineteenth century, and it reflected how strongly the past resonated for Harvey, who felt much more at home in the nineteenth than the twentieth century. Harvey once wrote that when his thoughts turned to New Mexico and his boyhood, "I feel that haunting, nostalgic sadness that lives in the long past—the sadness of vanished worlds, of former selves, of finished things living only in memory."[24]

Harvey brought what lived in memory to life, infusing many of his books with his New Mexican background, even though he moved to

Harvey Fergusson (left) with Witter Bynner, Taos, 1927.
Courtesy Palace of the Governors (MNM/DCA). Neg. no. 66421.

Berkeley in 1931. The 1933 *Rio Grande*, for example, his first nonfiction work, explored how the mighty river flowed from New Mexico's past into its future. He also wrote two books based on his own family history: *In Those Days: An Impression of Change*, a 1929 novel based on the life of his adventurous grandfather Franz Huning, and *Home in the West: An Inquiry into My Origins*, a 1945 autobiography.

Harvey covered other subjects, but he seemed most at home writing about his native state. His final novel, *The Conquest of Don Pedro*, became a Literary Guild selection upon publication in 1954, reaping Harvey his greatest financial success. The story about a non-violent Jewish merchant who establishes a shop in El Paso after the Civil War moved its readers with its focus on a thoughtful and gentle hero. Powell called it Harvey's "ripest book, his last harvest" because it was full of wisdom about the land and the people living between Albuquerque and El Paso.[25] When Harvey died in 1971 he had earned the title critics gave him during the last years of his life: the "dean of the Southwestern novelists."[26]

Paul Horgan: Venerated Historian

Paul Horgan never settled in Santa Fe or Taos, though he did spend time in both places. He wrote more than forty books, but most were published after 1950. Yet he established his literary career during the era of the Santa Fe and Taos writers' colonies and his books shed a powerful light on the history of the region. More prolific than any other writer examined in this book, he primarily wrote fiction and history, for which he won two Pulitzer prizes. He also worked in the genres of poetry, biography, drama, memoir, and children's stories. His biographer Robert Franklin Gish described him as "a writer's writer who wrote about the Southwest as well as the American East.[27]

Born in Buffalo, Horgan moved to Albuquerque at age twelve because the climate was good for his father's ill health. He attended Albuquerque High School, where his freshman English teacher happened to be Willa Cather's youngest sister, Elsie. The youthful Horgan must have found parallels to his feelings about leaving the East for the Southwest in the works of Willa Cather, whose writing echoed with the impact of moving from civilized Virginia to the untamed plains of Nebraska as a child. Perhaps those shared sentiments, which arose at such tender,

Paul Horgan, date unknown. Photo by Jill Krementz. Courtesy Center for Southwest Research, University Libraries, University of New Mexico. No. 000–478–0282 from the Alice Bullock Collection.

influential ages, are what propelled both writers to develop such a strong sense of place and a gift for writing about the land and the people connected to it.

Horgan spent nearly forty years in Roswell, where he became the librarian at the New Mexico Military Institute. In 1959, he moved to Middletown, Connecticut, to teach at Wesleyan University, but the Southwest had captured his heart. His extensive knowledge of the region's history and culture fills many of his works of fiction and nonfiction about New Mexico's three cultures—Native American, Hispano, and Anglo. Yet he also set some of his novels and short stories on the East Coast, in places in Pennsylvania and New York. His 1954 *Great River: The Rio Grande in North American History*, a weighty nonfiction tome that practically transforms the lifeblood of New Mexico into a virtual character, chronicles the history of the people who relied upon the Rio Grande and won a Pulitzer Prize for history. His 1975 biography *Lamy of Santa Fe: His Life and Times* also won the Pulitzer Prize for history. *The Centuries of Santa Fe*, published in 1956, traces three centuries of New Mexico history, beginning with the founding of Santa Fe in 1610.

Horgan was so adept at writing both fiction and history that he often merged the two genres. "The history one finds in Horgan's writings is always influenced by the truths of fiction," his biographer Gish wrote. *Great River* and *Lamy of Santa Fe* "are as much biography as history, as much novels as nonfiction narratives."[28] It is precisely this gift, which some critics have faulted for deviating from the facts, that has kept Horgan's work popular among contemporary readers. He died in 1995 in Middletown, having established himself as a writer who, like Cather, appealed to a universal audience even though he set much of his work in one region. He was highly skilled at writing about that region, and the people who occupied it, with a profound sensitivity for what it means to be human.

Fray Angélico Chávez: Gifted Storyteller

While the Anglo writers kept busy writing about New Mexico's distinct cultures they believed they "discovered" upon moving to the state, a small group of writers whose families had lived in the region for decades began to tell their stories too. Perhaps their motivation

Left to right, Fray Angélico Chávez, Sylvanus Morley,
Ernest L. Blumenschein. Photo by Robert Martin.
Courtesy Palace of the Governors (MNM/DCA). Negative no. 41361.

arose from watching the newcomers and reading their works. Even more likely, they may have simply wanted to share their stories with an audience of interested readers, no matter the background. Among this group, the treasured writings of Fray Angélico Chávez remain readily accessible and impressive to the general reader and scholar alike.

Born in Wagon Mound in 1910, Manuel Ezequiel Chávez went to a school run by the Sisters of Loretto in Mora. At age fourteen, he enrolled in the St. Francis Seminary in Cincinnati, Ohio, and became a Franciscan monk five years later, adopting the name Fray Angélico in homage to Fra Angelico da Fiesole, the medieval Italian painter. Chávez, too, was a talented painter who created murals and frescoes and labored to restore traditional church art in northern New Mexico. In 1937 he became a Franciscan priest, "the first native New Mexican ordained by the Franciscan Order."[29]

As he served in numerous New Mexico parishes and pueblo missions, he became devoted to scholarly research into New Mexico history's wide range of subjects, from the genealogies of Spanish Colonial families in old New Mexico to mission architecture, the Penitentes, and Padre Martínez. He also was a prolific writer of poetry and short stories who began publishing his work as teenager in the 1920s. During fifty years, he wrote five poetry collections, starting with *Clothed with the Sun*, a 1939 anthology of his devotional poems. T. S. Eliot praised the priest's 1959 book—*The Virgin of Port Lligat*, "a complex meditation on the metaphysics of the nuclear age"—as a "very commendable achievement."[30] Chávez also wrote bundles of short stories, sketches, and tales as well as an historical novel and an array of innovative works that echoed the triptychs of sacred art seen in traditional Spanish Colonial churches scattered across northern New Mexico.

In half a century, Chávez wrote piles of books and hundreds of poems, short stories, and articles related to Hispano culture in New Mexico. "Yet despite this outpouring of history, poetry, and fiction, Fray Angélico Chávez has been largely overlooked as one of the pioneers of Chicano literature in this century,"[31] lamented Genaro Padilla in his introduction to *The Short Stories of Fray Angélico Chávez*. The stories reveal a deep sensitivity to New Mexico's richly layered history.

The End of an Era

THE SANTA FE AND TAOS literary colonies began to fade in the late 1930s and ultimately disappeared with the outbreak of World War II. Before the colonies ended, however, their output reached readers around the region as well as across the country through publications that devoted countless pages to work from the Santa Fe and Taos colony writers.

The State Highway Department, for instance, debuted its official publication, *New Mexico Highway Journal*, in 1923 and by 1927 the magazine was publishing literary offerings from Frank Applegate and other authors. In 1931, the magazine merged with *Conservationist*, the State Game and Fish Department's official publication, to create a new publication, *New Mexico: The Sunshine State's Recreational and Highway Magazine*, which featured book reviews as well as literary pieces. (*New Mexico* later became the State Tourism Department's monthly *New Mexico Magazine*.)

While only a portion of *New Mexico*'s pages covered the literary realm, the *New Mexico Quarterly Review*, launched in 1931 by the University of New Mexico, entirely devoted itself to the state's literary community. It "was designed to give to the faculty, advanced students and all others who may have something worthwhile to contribute to the literature and scholarly thought of New Mexico an outlet for

145

Advertisement from *Laughing Horse*, no. 14, 1927.
Courtesy Gerald Peters Gallery Bookstore.

writing."[1] Many of the Santa Fe and Taos colony writers contributed
pieces to the journal and their books were reviewed in its pages. In 1929
the University of New Mexico launched its own press to publish books
related to the region.

Federal Aid for Literature

The Works Progress Administration, created in 1935 as a program of
Franklin Delano Roosevelt's New Deal, helped to extend the life of
the colonies during the Great Depression years by providing income
for writers. The New Mexico Federal Writers' Project, started in 1935
and renamed the New Mexico Writers' Program in 1939, lasted until
1943. Its primary offerings included a 1937 events calendar, printed
by the Rydal Press; a project devoted to the collection and translation
of Hispano folklore and folk life; and three books—*New Mexico: A
Guide to the Colorful State*, part of the American Guide series, published in 1940; *New Mexico*, published in 1941 as part of the American

Recreational Series; and *The Spanish-American Song and Game Book*, published in 1942. When World War II intervened, subsequent projects in the works had to be scrapped.

Signs that the colonies had begun to erode predated the war, however. By the mid-1930s, many of the Santa Fe and Taos literary figures began to wonder whether their decision to live in, and write about, a region far removed from mainstream America and the East Coast literary establishment had doomed them to obscurity. While new writers continued to make Santa Fe and Taos their homes, few "had the stature and innovative vision of the founding mothers and fathers and the best of the 1920s visitors."[2]

The Los Alamos Legacy

With the outbreak of World War II, the writers' colonies slid into a rapid demise as numerous people left to serve their country and volunteer for various war efforts. Top-secret work on the atomic bomb that began in 1943 in Los Alamos, about thirty miles northwest of Santa Fe, brought the country's leading physicists and scientists to the "city on the hill." After their creations destroyed the Japanese cities of Hiroshima and Nagasaki, the notion of New Mexico as a sanctuary—a remote outpost where creative people could escape the modern world—vanished almost instantly. Beneath the shadow of such destructive forces, many of the writers who stayed found much less inspiration in the beauty of the landscape and the wealth of cultures that had drawn them to the Southwest in the first place. They must have felt overwhelmed by the strange balance of power that suddenly descended on their desert, juxtaposing the ancestors of an ancient, indigenous culture that revered every aspect of nature with a scientific laboratory that produced weapons capable of eradicating all of nature and scores of human lives.

The postwar years opened northern New Mexico up to the same forces of "progress" that marched through the rest of America. As Frank Waters described it in 1951,

> World War II abruptly ended the period with the great influx of new residents. The beauty of the valley, the slow tempo of the Spanish-American villages, and the rhythmic appeal of Pueblo life have given way to the ruthless demands of economic development and

commercial exploitation. Art is no longer paramount. The super-
market, the filling station, the travel folder and highway billboards
advertise Taos as no different than any other spot in America.[3]

Nabokov in New Mexico

Still the myth of northern New Mexico persisted, continuing to lure
literary figures long after the writers' colonies had faded. Vladimir
Nabokov, for instance, spent two months in Taos in a rented adobe
with his wife, Vera, and son, Dmitri, during the summer of 1954. His
experience, however, hardly matched what other writers felt about Taos
before him. Drawn by the allure of an adobe house with an orchard
and gardens ten miles from Taos and renting for the summer for just
$250, the family drove their "frog-green Buick" to Taos from Ithaca,
New York, where Nabokov was teaching at Cornell University.[4] Upon
arrival, however, the Russian author was dismayed to discover he had
been duped. Instead of pastoral peace, the family found a renter's night-
mare. Their new home squatted next to a road with nothing but a tiny
garden plot behind it.

> There was nowhere to walk or even sit outside in privacy. The
> promised rushing mountain river was an irrigation ditch. They did
> not care for the 'painful quaintness' of the house. Dust and sand
> drifted down constantly from the ceiling. Mice droppings littered
> shelves and drawers. Flies buzzed in through the doors and faulty
> screens. In a south wind the smell of the sewer pervaded the house.
> At first they wanted to flee immediately, but then decided to see if
> they could stick it out.[5]

The family gave Taos a try, but Nabokov soon decided the town was
nothing but "a dismal hole full of third-rate painters and faded pansies,"
and "an ugly and dreary town with soi-disant 'picturesque' Indian pau-
pers placed at strategic points by the Chamber of Commerce to lure
tourists from Oklahoma and Texas who deem the place 'arty.'"[6] He
did, though, enjoy discovering "interesting butterflies" in the nearby
canyons with Dmitri, who drove him there "in a World War II jeep
that came with the house."[7] Even that brief joy died when the whole
family took ill, following the drowning of two animals that made their

way into the water tank. When their corpses decomposed, Nabokov's wife became so sick she was rushed to an Albuquerque doctor, whose "diagnosis of her liver condition was so alarming" that he sent her by train to her New York doctors, who decided, after her arrival, that she had recovered. Nabokov described the entire Taos experience as a "hectic hash of a summer."[8]

The Hippie Happening

When a later countercultural movement took root in America during the 1960s and 1970s, Santa Fe and Taos drew large groups of hippies who, like Mabel Dodge Luhan and her friends before them, developed an interest in Pueblo Indian practices and beliefs. Even then, serious writers continued to trek to the region. Edward Abbey, widely considered to be "the Thoreau of the American West," was an Easterner by birth but the ties he forged with the Southwest made him an ardent advocate for protecting and preserving the environment, a major tenet of the hippie generation.[9]

A graduate of the University of New Mexico, Abbey wrote more than twenty novels and essays—work that "veers from passionate paeans to the earth to strident demands for its protection."[10] Years after his death in 1989, Abbey remains the focus of college classes around the country. He has earned a cult following among people who still believe that his death was a hoax, insisting that they have just sighted him somewhere in the vast desert landscape of the American Southwest. Abbey's novel *The Brave Cowboy*, published in 1956, was adapted in 1962 as the screen classic *Lonely Are the Brave*, starring Kirk Douglas. His 1968 nonfiction book *Desert Solitaire*, based on his experiences as a Utah park ranger, remains a cult classic too.

Abbey's passion for the environment undeniably influenced many subsequent writers of the region, including John Nichols, who moved to Taos in 1969 after the 1965 publication of his acclaimed first novel, *The Sterile Cuckoo*. Nichols's 1974 novel *The Milagro Beanfield War* became another best-selling book about New Mexico. The story blends magical realism with the moving plight of one man's fight to save his family farm from real-estate developers. The tale remains true for many New Mexican families facing a similar battle today.

Capote and Sinister Spiders

Southern author Truman Capote reportedly rented a Santa Fe house for the summer of 1976 with a married man, John O'Shea, his then companion who also served as Capote's manager.[11] Capote paid for the lease in advance but, following an argument with O'Shea, departed so quickly that he left behind a wealth of material in the house, including two handwritten manuscripts and a note from Ben Bradlee, then the *Washington Post*'s editor.

Capote might well have read, and thoroughly enjoyed, *The Spider in the Cup*, a 1955 infamous mystery written by Norman Hales and published by Signet Books, which billed it on the back pulp fiction cover as a story "pulsating with violence and raw emotion . . . an explosive thriller about a sinister woman, whose unbridled passion wreaks havoc among the artists and writers in a colorful Southwestern Bohemia." Southwestern Bohemia actually was a stand-in for Santa Fe, and Hales was a pseudonym for "a well-known movie critic who has lived for many years in Santa Fe."[12] The writer's real name reportedly was Vernon Young, according to a cheat sheet that has circulated for years among Santa Fe book dealers, bibliophiles, and residents, who expressed outrage at the send-up of the "Arty Colony" of Santa Fe. The cast of characters may have been drawn from real-life literary and art figures. The book seems to have disappeared from local library shelves and bookstores, but at least a few readers have surely held onto their copies for nostalgic or nefarious reasons.

Literary Legacies

In the early twenty-first century, Santa Fe—with a population approaching seventy thousand—holds the distinction of being the country's second largest art market. Taos has grown also, with a population of about five thousand. Both Santa Fe and Taos have healthy communities of writers working in every genre, from poets to cult novelists, best-selling mystery writers, biographers, award-winning cookbook authors, Jungian scholars, historians, essayists, children's book authors, and spiritual and self-help writers. Numerous groups devoted to the literary arts, such as the prestigious Lannan Foundation, serve both communities as well. Best of all, the eclectic range of writers who live and work in the region rivals the number of literary lions of the colony era. Acclaimed poets such as Arthur Sze, Jon Davis, Miriam Sagan, Joan Logghe, Dana Levin, Nathaniel Tarn, Greg Glazner, Gary Mex Glazner, Valerie Martinez, Jimmy Santiago Baca, and Joe Ray Sandoval are inspired by the same landscape and cultures as celebrated authors Frederick Turner and Lisa Tucker, cult novelist Evan S. Connell, and successful mystery writers Sarah Lovett and David Morrell, who makes his home here but writes about a dizzying range of subjects. Even Cormac McCarthy spends a lot of time in New Mexico's high desert. An increasing number of emerging authors have found their way here as well. Clearly, northern New Mexico continues to cast its spell on those who work magic with words.

Walking/Driving Tours

A VISIT TO some of the houses, gathering spots, and public spaces once occupied by members of the Santa Fe and Taos writers' colonies can vividly bring the era of the 1920s and 1930s to life. In many cases, the homes have been well preserved or restored by later owners who converted them to inns. Most of the new owners have collected a combination of history and legend about the former owners that they enthusiastically share with guests. Not all of their stories are true, though. Surely the claims in New Mexico that "D. H. Lawrence slept here" have become almost as common as the claims in New Jersey that "George Washington slept here."

Out of respect for privacy, this tour presents only those places in Santa Fe and Taos that the public can visit, omitting, for example, homes that belonged to Alice Corbin Henderson and Oliver La Farge, which remain private residences. And while many of the tour sites can be reached on foot, not all of the stops are close together. Visits to Bishop's Lodge, the Lamy depot, and the D. H. Lawrence ranch require a vehicle.

Santa Fe

Mary Austin's House, 438 Camino del Monte Sol
This handsome adobe, now housing the Chiaroscuro Gallery, an art

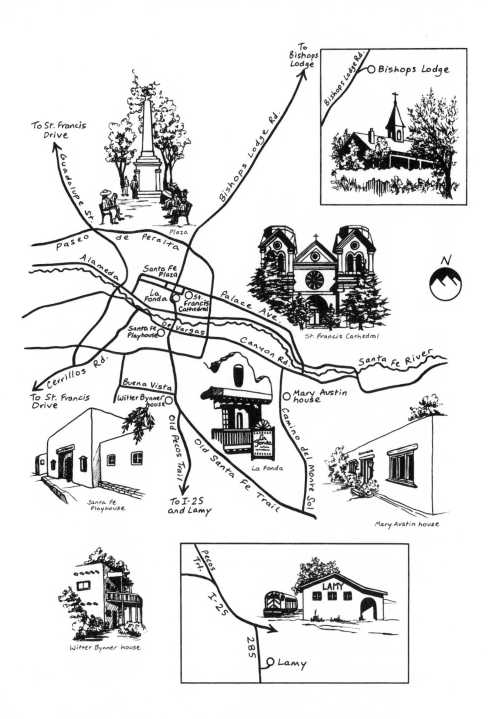

Walking/Driving Tour of Santa Fe, created by Shirley Lynn.

gallery, was built in 1924 as the residence of Mary Austin, a self-proclaimed mystic and prolific author of novels, poetry, essays, and nonfiction books devoted to feminism, human ecology, and other topics well ahead of her time.

For construction and design, Austin enlisted the help of her neighbor Frank Applegate, an artist, architect, and expert collector of Native American and Spanish Colonial art. Austin persuaded Applegate to record and publish the stories of the people whose art he collected. Austin herself collected Native American pottery and textiles, and her pieces now belong to the School of American Research in Santa Fe. Guests in her home included esteemed American author Willa Cather, who may have written the final pages of her classic novel *Death Comes for the Archbishop* in Austin's library.

Throughout her life, Austin lived in many places, from Carmel, California, to New York City, and she traveled extensively. Yet she ultimately decided to settle in Santa Fe, where she spent the last decade of her life. She called her adobe home Casa Querida (Spanish for "Beloved Home"), and invited others to enjoy the space she cherished, hosting intellectual gatherings, readings, and a school of fine arts.

Witter Bynner's House, 342 Buena Vista Street

Nearly three years after Witter Bynner moved to Santa Fe in 1922 and rented a three-room adobe from artist Paul Burlin, he purchased the property, which included an outside shack he converted to a writing studio. He then began an expansion that lasted almost forty years, initially financed by selling manuscripts to three O. Henry short stories, which the writer had given him to repay a loan. Thereafter, Bynner referred to the second-story addition, which included a covered porch, as the O. Henry Story. He also added bedrooms, a library for entertaining guests, and a music room.

After Bynner and Robert Hunt began their relationship in 1930, expansion of the house continued. Hunt, son of prominent California architect Myron Hunt, designed a second-story bedroom and bathroom for himself, along with a garage and an outside study on the west side. In 1963, Hunt added three more rooms that connected to the new study, thereby creating a truly rambling adobe.

The interior of Bynner's residence reflected the poet's fascination with the cultures of Asia and the Southwest. He filled his house with

Chinese, Native American, and Spanish Colonial art, including santos, Pueblo pottery, Navajo textiles, and Chinese porcelain and jade. He also collected guests, and before his death in 1968, an astounding number of noteworthy people from around the world had visited his house, attending his famous parties or merely sharing a meal with the poet. The impressive list included film stars Errol Flynn and Rita Hayworth, who stopped by during the 1940 world premiere of their Western film *Santa Fe Trail* in Santa Fe, as well as dancer Martha Graham, photographer Ansel Adams, and poet Robert Frost. D. H. Lawrence and Frieda spent their first night in New Mexico as guests in Bynner's house, and Bynner describes the encounter memorably in his 1951 book *Journey with Genius*, which chronicles Bynner's turbulent relationship with Lawrence.

Bynner's house is now the Inn of the Turquoise Bear, and its owners are happy to share their knowledge of Bynner's life and give tours of the property to guests and visitors.

Santa Fe Playhouse, 142 East De Vargas Street

During her first visit to Santa Fe in 1918, author Mary Austin founded the Community Theatre to showcase local productions that reflected the Anglo, Hispano, and Native American cultures of the region. The debut production featured songs and plays in Spanish and English with stage sets designed by Santa Fe artists Gustave Baumann and Carlos Vierra. The following year, the theater company officially incorporated as the Santa Fe Little Theatre and has remained in business ever since, though the group has changed its name to the Santa Fe Playhouse.

Although this theater is not the original site of the Community Theatre's productions, the Santa Fe Playhouse has used the building since 1961 to continue the tradition Austin established of presenting plays and other performances that celebrate the diverse cultural community of Santa Fe.

Santa Fe Plaza, center of historic downtown Santa Fe, bordered by San Francisco Street and Washington, Palace, and Lincoln avenues

The plaza has been the heart of downtown since King Philip II of Spain ordered its construction in 1610 with the founding of Santa Fe. When the Santa Fe Trail opened in 1821, it led directly into the plaza, where wagons loaded with goods would flood into the square, having reached the end of their journey. The first fiesta took place on the plaza in 1712 as a celebration of the Spanish reconquest of the Pueblo Indians. During subsequent years, it faded as an annual event, but the writers and artists of the colony era helped revitalize the fiesta with new events so that it more accurately reflected the city's multicultural diversity instead of focusing solely on the Spanish defeat of the Pueblo people. For instance, the writers and artists created the "hysterical-historical parade," which included outrageous costumes and buffoonery. Witter Bynner, who led the parade with artist John Sloan's wife, Dolly, dressed one year as a diapered baby. During the 1920s and 1930s, the writers and artists joined the crowds on the plaza for the annual fiesta celebrations, an early September tradition that continues to this day.

La Fonda, 100 East San Francisco Street, on the Santa Fe Plaza

Santa Fe's oldest hotel was the main gathering spot for the writers of the colony era and just about everybody else in town. Opened in 1920, La Fonda quickly became a landmark for its Spanish Pueblo Revival architecture and its elegant restaurant, bar, and meeting rooms. Fred Harvey took over in 1925 and transformed La Fonda into one of his famous Harvey Hotels, hiring acclaimed Santa Fe architect John Gaw Meem to expand the property from 46 to 156 rooms. Celebrated Harvey House designer Mary Colter created the interior, filling the hotel with antique Mexican and hand-carved Spanish Colonial furniture, Pueblo pottery, Navajo rugs, and other Southwestern accents. Willa Cather rented guest rooms in the hotel during several of her stays in Santa Fe, and the Santa Fe writers and artists hosted an annual masquerade ball in the hotel that changed themes each year. In 1932, for instance, the Jungle Ball drew about five hundred guests costumed as missionaries, monkeys, explorers, and tribal natives wearing grass skirts, feathers, and plenty of grease paint.

Saint Francis Cathedral, one block east of the
Plaza on Cathedral Place and San Francisco Street

Archbishop Jean Baptiste Lamy, New Mexico's first archbishop, ordered the construction of the stone cathedral in 1869. The design incorporated French Gothic and Romanesque architectural styles with stained glass windows imported from France. Before the chapel was dedicated in 1886, however, the funding had run out, so the spires were never completed. The cathedral was built on top of an adobe church that had served the community for two hundred years. Once the cathedral's construction was completed, the adobe church was torn down, except for the chapel, which still exists in the cathedral's northeast side.

In front of the cathedral's main doors stands a bronze statue depicting Lamy. The statue sparked Willa Cather's imagination as she first conceived of the story line for her classic 1927 novel *Death Comes for the Archbishop*, while staying at La Fonda across the street in the summer of 1925. Lamy's grave lies beneath the cathedral's main altar.

The Bishop's Lodge, 3¹/₂ miles north of Santa Fe on Bishop's Lodge Road

Archbishop Jean Baptiste Lamy, a native of France, arrived in New Mexico in 1851 to become the first bishop for the Vatican's new diocese of Santa Fe, representing New Mexico, Arizona, Colorado, and parts of Utah. Even before he was appointed archbishop in 1875, the vast scope of his job led him to create a simple retreat in the serene foothills north of Santa Fe, along the Little Tesuque Stream. On a plot of land purchased from Spanish Colonial settlers during the 1860s, Lamy built a small, unadorned chapel flanked by two rooms—a sitting room and a bedroom that also contained an office. He established gardens planted with lilac and fruit trees—some of which he imported from France—and a pond filled with fish. He often invited guests to enjoy his sanctuary, offering Mass in his chapel and a meal in his sitting room. He called his retreat Villa Pintoresca (Italian for "Picturesque Villa"), though the portal and adobe walls of the building reflect traditional New Mexican architecture.

After Lamy died in 1888, the property passed through several owners until a Denver businessman bought it and turned it into a resort in 1918. The current corporate owner recently renovated the property into the Bishop's Lodge Resort & Spa, but Lamy's chapel remains relatively unchanged and is open to the public. One important visitor, Willa Cather, found great inspiration viewing Lamy's chapel during her stay in Santa Fe in 1925 while researching her classic novel about a fictionalized Lamy.

Lamy, nine miles southeast of Santa Fe via I-25 north to U.S. 285 south

The railroad arrived in New Mexico in 1880 but because of elevation and tricky terrain, the main line completely bypassed Santa Fe, despite the name of its owner—the Atchison, Topeka & Santa Fe Railroad Company.

Lamy became the line's official stop, from which an eighteen-mile spur connected railroad travelers to Santa Fe. Formerly a sheep-grazing locale for Spanish settlers that belonged to a land grant Archbishop Jean Baptiste Lamy purchased for the church, Lamy became a real railroad town, complete with a luxurious Harvey House hotel that opened in 1910. The El Ortiz, a one-story Pueblo Revival structure with an interior created by famed Harvey House designer Mary Colter, hosted noteworthy guests, including William "Buffalo Bill" Cody, before it closed in 1939 and was demolished sometime in the 1940s. After the Santa Fe Railway shut down the branch line into Santa Fe in 1926, a Harvey Car carried passengers into town.

Many of the writers who visited or settled in Santa Fe and Taos during the 1920s and 1930s took in their first views of northern New Mexico while stepping off the train at this depot. Today the Santa Fe Southern Railway runs historic train cars from Santa Fe to Lamy on the railroad's original branch line. The round-trip tours depart from the downtown Santa Fe Depot on Guadalupe Street. The trip takes several hours, as opposed to a typical twenty-minute drive, but passengers can experience a journey through time as they travel the same path taken by the early colony writers. No longer a bustling train stop, the sparsely-populated town of Lamy is rather lonely. Like the Atchison, Topeka & Santa Fe line before it, the Amtrak stops at Lamy, but travelers still have to arrange transportation into Santa Fe, just as the writers did eighty years ago.

Taos

Willard "Spud" Johnson's House, 729 Paseo del Pueblo Norte
When Spud Johnson moved to Taos from Santa Fe in the late 1920s, he brought his small, satirical magazine, *Laughing Horse*, with him. He eventually settled in what was then a modest adobe built in the late nineteenth century by the banks of the Rio Pueblo, where he lived until his death in 1968. During Johnson's occupancy, the house had just a few rooms, including a kitchen with a mud floor and a bathroom that doubled as a morning room when Johnson placed a wooden board covered with a Native American blanket over the bathtub, creating a place to sit and, presumably, to write and edit. Johnson added a living room by building around an old covered well, which became a coffee table in a living room crowded with books, magazines, and a foot-powered

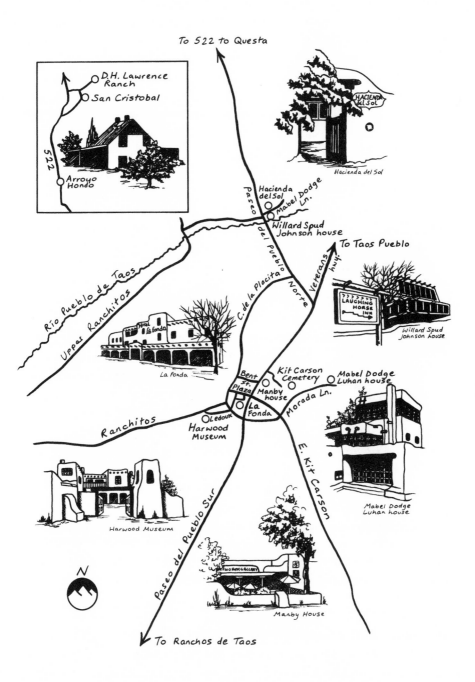

Walking/Driving Tour of Taos, created by Shirley Lynn.

printing press in one corner that issued *Laughing Horse*, pamphlets, and a weekly one-sheet newspaper about amusing or noteworthy events in Taos called *The Horse Fly*.

After Johnson died, a medical doctor purchased the property and added on a winding wing of small examining rooms. Later, someone added a second-story loft. Today the building is an eclectic bed and breakfast aptly named The Laughing Horse Inn, which appeals to people seeking offbeat, alternative accommodations in much the same way that *Laughing Horse* attracted readers interested in unconventional viewpoints.

Hacienda del Sol, 109 Mabel Dodge Lane, off Paseo del Pueblo Norte

This elegant adobe house that overlooks Taos Mountain dates to 1804. More than a century later, Mabel Dodge Luhan took ownership and used it as one of her many guesthouses. In her day, the house had four rooms and an apple orchard on its extensive grounds. The proximity of Spud Johnson's former house may explain why, as editor of *Laughing Horse*, he was able to persuade some of Luhan's noteworthy guests to contribute to his magazine. Frank Waters reportedly stayed in this house while writing his 1941 novel *People of the Valley*. Local lore has it that other notables bunked here as well, including D. H. Lawrence. Today the house is a romantic inn with original wood plank floors, multiple fireplaces, and heavy vigas that, during Luhan's era, must have helped create a stimulating sanctuary for creativity.

Kit Carson Historic Cemetery, 211 Paseo del Pueblo Norte

Stroll past the large gravestones with commemorative text that mark the burial sites of trapper, scout, Indian agent, and soldier Kit Carson, and Padre Antonio José Martínez, credited with printing the first book in New Mexico, to the cemetery's southwest corner. There, a small, simple gravestone indicates Mabel Dodge Luhan's resting place. She was buried next to her Taos friend Ralph Meyers, the inspiration for Rodolfo Byers, the Indian trader in *The Man Who Killed the Deer*, the 1942 novel by Frank Waters. The text on a plaque near her grave credits Luhan's major role in creating an international reputation for the Taos art community and notes only in passing that she entertained many authors as well. However, the acclaim earned by authors who lived in or visited Taos at her urging proves that she also played a leading role in establishing a legitimate writers' colony.

Arthur Rochford Manby's House, 133 Paseo del Pueblo Norte

In *Edge of Taos Desert*, the fourth and final volume of her memoir, Mabel Dodge Luhan describes in vivid detail the run-down rooms she rented in this house from eccentric Englishman Arthur Manby when she first moved to Taos in 1917. Luhan was convinced that Manby had lost his mind after his schemes to establish a New Mexico land empire had failed. His bizarre death remains one of the big unsolved mysteries of the last century in Taos. In 1929, police discovered a headless body in his bedroom and presumed it was Manby's corpse. Other Taos residents, however, were convinced that the unscrupulous Manby had faked his own death to escape the wrath of people he had swindled. Frank Waters examines Manby's life, and death, in his 1973 biography *To Possess the Land*. Today an art gallery occupies Manby's former house. His grave lies in the Kit Carson Cemetery, not far from where Mabel Dodge Luhan is buried.

Mabel Dodge Luhan's House, 250 Morada Lane

Los Gallos, the formidable estate built by Taos arts patron, author, and socialite Mabel Dodge Luhan, takes its Spanish name ("The Chickens") from the row of colorful Mexican ceramic chickens perched along the lower roof. The statues, however, are not what most visitors notice first. What jumps out instead is the impressive house, which Luhan and her husband began building in 1918 after purchasing twelve acres and a five-room adobe house. Over the next decade, the original house was renovated and expanded in the Pueblo style of architecture, also known as Spanish Revival, to reflect some elements of the multistoried architecture of nearby Taos Pueblo.

The first room added was the Big Room, a formal gathering spot dominated by a large, square fireplace. The room contained European and Oriental furniture, Native American blankets displayed on the walls, and fresh roses and other flowers favored by Luhan. Her spacious bedroom occupied a second story above the Big Room and later, an enclosed sun porch was added as a third story, towering above a sprawling stone courtyard and overlooking the four directions held sacred by Pueblo Indians. A grand dining room built off of one end of the Big Room contained French windows providing ample natural light and a ceiling with painted stripes that resembled a Native American blanket. Off the other end of the Big Room stretched a wing of guest rooms accessed beneath a long portal. Mabel also added a library off the Big Room where she spent time writing. D. H. Lawrence painted the colorful windows enclosing the second story bathroom.

When the main residence, known as the Big House, reached completion, it had seventeen rooms occupying more than eight thousand square feet as well as a separate residence for servants. For Luhan, this simply wasn't enough space for the dozens of influential guests from around the world who visited her, including writers D. H. Lawrence, Willa Cather, Thornton Wilder, and Robinson Jeffers, as well as painter Georgia O'Keeffe, photographer Ansel Adams, and dancer Martha Graham. In order to accommodate her noteworthy visitors, she built five guesthouses on the property.

Los Gallos has changed little since Luhan's heyday and the current owners, who operate it as The Mabel Dodge Luhan House, an inn and conference center, strive to keep it that way.

Harwood Museum of Art, 238 Ledoux Street

Artist Burt Harwood and his wife, Elizabeth, left France in 1917 to move to Taos, where they purchased a home built in the mid-nineteenth century by Captain Smith Simpson, a U.S. army veteran and friend to Kit Carson. The Harwoods quickly turned their residence into a gathering spot for artists and writers. In 1923, shortly after Burt Harwood's death, his wife established the Harwood Foundation as an art and community center with a public library. Mabel Dodge Luhan donated a large collection of best-selling and classic books as well as finances to help launch the library, which in its early years consisted of a lending library that Elizabeth Harwood ran from her front porch.

Before her death, Elizabeth Harwood arranged for the University of New Mexico to take over the foundation in 1935, and John Gaw Meem, the acclaimed pioneer of Spanish Pueblo revival architecture, spent the next few years renovating and expanding the Harwood home. The foundation became a central part of the cultural community of Taos, hosting art exhibits, plays, concerts, and classes, and amassing an impressive collection of art, including Pueblo pottery, Spanish Colonial art, and works by the Taos Society of Artists. The foundation's board members included writers Spud Johnson and Peggy Pond Church. Mabel Dodge Luhan gifted the group her collection of nineteenth-century santos.

Today the complex is called the Harwood Museum of Art of the

University of New Mexico. It is devoted to historic and contemporary art of the region. Although the public library has since relocated from the Harwood compound, the Southwest Research Center of Northern New Mexico—housed in a wing of the Harwood—offers a rich archive of publications and other information about an array of history subjects connected to Taos and the Southwest.

La Fonda de Taos, 108 South Plaza

An inn has occupied this spot on the plaza since 1820, but the building has changed hands numerous times. In 1937, two Greek brothers, James and John Karavas, bought the Colombian Hotel & Bar, a Pueblo Revival–style building, and renovated the property, adding two stories and renaming it La Fonda de Taos. The son of one of those brothers, Saki Karavas, ran the hotel from 1953 until his death in 1996.

La Fonda de Taos may be the unlikeliest place to stumble across oil paintings by British author D. H. Lawrence, who began to experiment with painting at age forty, just four years before he died. The hotel's former owner has a history, however, that explains how the paintings ended up there.

An avid art collector who knew Mabel Dodge Luhan and Frieda Lawrence, Saki Karavas purchased nine of Lawrence's oil paintings from Angelo Ravagli, who married Lawrence's widow, Frieda, in 1950 and settled with her on the Kiowa Ranch property north of Taos. The sale took place in 1956, after Frieda's death, and Karavas began exhibiting the paintings in his hotel office, charging visitors a few dollars to view them.

The current hotel owners have set aside a small gallery in La Fonda for the Lawrence paintings and the current three-dollar admission fee hasn't gone up much since Saki's day. The hotel bills the nine paintings as "Forbidden Art" because in 1929—when Lawrence's novel *Lady Chatterley's Lover* had already been banned for containing obscene material—police confiscated the works to prevent them from being exhibited to the public in a London gallery. London society, it seems, was just not ready to view oil paintings with nude figures. By today's standards, the paintings would hardly offend viewers except, perhaps, serious art connoisseurs, who most likely will be disappointed by Lawrence's skills as a painter.

La Fonda de Taos also served as a gathering spot for many of the Taos artists and writers, including Mabel Dodge Luhan.

***D. H. Lawrence Ranch, San Cristobal, NM (take Route 522 north toward
Questa, turn right at the sign for D. H. Lawrence Ranch
before San Cristobal, and follow signs to the ranch)***

D. H. Lawrence visited New Mexico with his wife, Frieda, three times
between 1922 and 1926. During the second and third visit, the couple lived at the ranch that Lawrence alternately called Lobo Ranch,
presumably after the wolves that prowled the pristine wilderness, and
Kiowa Ranch, after an ancient Native American trail used by Kiowa
Indians. Mabel Dodge Luhan had purchased the property for her son
but she gave it to the Lawrences in exchange for D. H. Lawrence's manuscript of *Sons and Lovers*.

The Lawrences stayed at the ranch from May to October 1924 and
then again from April to September 1925, occupying the homesteader's cabin that dated to the late nineteenth century. The rustic cabin
had no electricity or running water, but Lawrence found inspiration to
write when he wasn't tending chickens, riding horses, and fixing up
the property. The Lawrences had to make improvements to the cabin,
which was in a state of disrepair when they took occupancy. They gave
a smaller cabin on the ranch to Dorothy Brett, an Englishwoman who
accompanied the Lawrences to New Mexico in 1924 hoping to join the
utopian community that Lawrence envisioned but never established.
Brett, a painter, was devoted to Lawrence, and ended up spending the
rest of her life in New Mexico.

After Lawrence died in 1940, his widow returned to the cabin with
her Italian lover, Angelo Ravagli, who built a memorial shrine. The
shrine held Lawrence's ashes once his body had been disinterred from
his grave in Vence, France; cremated; and brought to America. Frieda
died in 1956, and she was buried outside of the shrine, her grave marked
by a white marble slab.

Today the ranch is owned by the University of New Mexico, which
rents out cabins on the property to university students, staff, and alumni
only. The memorial shrine, however, is open to the public. The ranch's
rich legacy has earned it a deserved spot on the National Register of
Historic Places.

Notes

Introduction

1. T. M. Pearce, *Alice Corbin Henderson* (Austin, TX: Steck-Vaughn Co., 1969), 13.
2. Paul Horgan, *The Centuries of Santa Fe* (Albuquerque: University of New Mexico Press, 1994), ix.
3. Lois Palken Rudnick, *Utopian Vistas: The Mabel Dodge Luhan House and the American Counterculture* (Albuquerque: University of New Mexico Press, 1996), 24.
4. From Karal Ann Marling's introduction to *Woodstock: An American Art Colony, 1902–1977* (Poughkeepsie, NY: Vassar College Art Gallery, 1977), n.p.

Chapter One

1. Alice Corbin Henderson, "Literature," *New Mexico: A Guide to the Colorful State* (New York: Hastings House, 1940), 130.
2. Horgan, *The Centuries of Santa Fe*, 18.
3. Ibid., 3.
4. Rudolfo Anaya, *Serafina's Stories* (Albuquerque: University of New Mexico Press, 2004), 199.
5. Philip Stevenson, "Santa Fe: A Study in Integrity," *New Mexico Quarterly Review*, August 1933, 128.
6. Henderson, "Literature," 131.
7. Ibid., 132.
8. Ibid.
9. Pamela S. Smith with Richard Polese, *Passions in Print: Private Press Artistry in New Mexico, 1834–Present* (Santa Fe: Museum of New Mexico Press, 2006), 21.

10. Ibid.

11. Mabel Dodge Luhan, *Edge of Taos Desert* (1937; repr., Albuquerque: University of New Mexico Press, 1987), 85.

12. Henderson, "Literature," 132.

13. William P. Barrett, "The Curse of Lew Wallace" (*Crosswinds Weekly*, May 1998), expanded Internet version at members.aol.com/wmpb2/CrossWallace.

14. Marta Weigle and Kyle Fiore, *Santa Fe and Taos: The Writer's Era, 1916–1941* (Santa Fe: Ancient City Press, 1982), 5.

15. Phyllis Cole Braunlich, *Haunted by Home: The Life and Letters of Lynn Riggs* (Norman: University of Oklahoma Press, 1988), 138.

16. Ibid., 139.

17. Weigle and Fiore, *Santa Fe and Taos*, 157.

18. Ibid.

19. Oliver La Farge, *The Man with the Calabash Pipe* (Boston: Houghton Mifflin, 1966), 8.

20. Smith, *Passions in Print*, 41.

Chapter Two

1. From Rudnick's introduction to Alice Corbin Henderson, *Red Earth, Poems of New Mexico*, comp. and ed. Lois Rudnick and Ellen Zieselman (Chicago: Ralph Fletcher Seymour, 1920; Santa Fe: Museum of New Mexico Press, 2003), 20.

2. Ibid., 13.

3. Pearce, *Alice Corbin Henderson*, 13.

4. Ibid.

5. From Rudnick's introduction to Henderson, *Red Earth*, 13.

6. Weigle and Fiore, *Santa Fe and Taos*, 22.

7. From Rudnick's introduction to Henderson, *Red Earth*, 21.

8. Ibid., 25.

9. Ibid., 23.

10. Ibid.

11. Ibid., 26.

12. Ibid., 37.

13. Weigle and Fiore, *Santa Fe and Taos*, 19.

14. Alice Corbin Henderson, *The Turquoise Trail: An Anthology of New Mexico Poetry* (Boston: Houghton Mifflin, 1928), ix.

15. Weigle and Fiore, *Santa Fe and Taos*, 39.

16. Pearce, *Alice Corbin Henderson*, 31.

17. See Smith, *Passions in Print*, 56–62, for the information in this section on Goodwin and the Rydal Press.

18. Henderson, "Literature," 130.

19. From Rudnick introduction to *Red Earth*, 32.

20. Witter Bynner, "Alice and I," *New Mexico Quarterly Review*, Spring 1949, 42.

Chapter Three

1. Weigle and Fiore, *Santa Fe and Taos*, 80.
2. James Kraft, *Who Is Witter Bynner?* (Albuquerque: University of New Mexico Press, 1995), 16.
3. Ibid., 36.
4. Ibid.
5. Ibid., 37.
6. Ibid., 38.
7. Ibid., 41.
8. Ibid., 39.
9. Ibid.
10. Ibid., 38.
11. Ibid., 44.
12. Witter Bynner, *The Selected Witter Bynner: Poems, Plays, Translations, Prose and Letters*, ed. James Kraft (Albuquerque: University of New Mexico Press, 1995), 83.
13. Kraft, *Who Is Witter Bynner?*, 98.
14. Bynner, "Alice and I," 36.
15. Kraft, *Who Is Witter Bynner?*, 49.
16. Bynner, "Alice and I," 37.
17. Kraft, *Who Is Witter Bynner?*, 50.
18. Ibid., 51.
19. Ibid., 87.
20. Bynner, "Alice and I," 38.
21. Raymond Otis, *Fire in the Night* (New York: Farrar and Rinehart, 1934), 26.
22. Kraft, *Who Is Witter Bynner?*, 53.
23. Ibid., 52.
24. See ibid., 55, for all quotes about *Cake* in this paragraph.
25. See Lois Palken Rudnick, *Mabel Dodge Luhan: New Woman, New Worlds* (1984; Albuquerque: University of New Mexico Press, 2000), 328, for anecdotes and quotes in this paragraph.
26. Witter Bynner, *Journey with Genius: Recollections and Reflections Concerning the D. H. Lawrences* (New York: John Day, 1951), 300.
27. Ibid., 306.
28. D. H. Lawrence, *The Plumed Serpent (Quetzalcoatl)* (New York: Alfred A. Knopf, 1926), 10.
29. Kraft, *Who Is Witter Bynner?*, 54.
30. Ibid., 64.
31. Ibid., 104.
32. Ibid., 106.
33. Ibid.
34. Ibid., 60.
35. Bynner, *The Selected Witter Bynner*, 72.

Chapter Four

1. Esther Lanigan Stineman, *Mary Austin: Song of a Maverick* (New Haven: Yale University Press, 1989), 4.
2. Ibid., 18.
3. Mary Austin, *Earth Horizon* (Boston: Houghton Mifflin, 1932), 294.
4. Ibid., 257.
5. Stineman, *Mary Austin*, 5.
6. Ibid., 71.
7. Rudnick, *Utopian Vistas*, 89.
8. Lawrence Clark Powell, *Southwest Classics* (1974; Pasadena: Ward Ritchie Press, 1975), 95.
9. Stineman, *Mary Austin*, 154.
10. Ibid., 155.
11. Austin, *Earth Horizon*, 354.
12. Mary Austin, "Frank Applegate," *New Mexico Quarterly Review*, August 1932, 216.
13. Stineman, *Mary Austin*, 153.
14. Ibid., 161.
15. Austin, *Earth Horizon*, 355.
16. Rudnick, *Utopian Vistas*, 91.
17. Ibid.
18. Austin, *Earth Horizon*, 33.
19. Mary Austin, *Land of Little Rain* (1903; New York: Dover Publications, 1996), 8.

Chapter Five

1. Sharon O'Brien, *Willa Cather: The Emerging Voice* (New York: Ballantine, 1989), 59.
2. Ibid., 60.
3. Ibid.
4. Ibid., 346.
5. Elizabeth Shepley Sergeant, *Willa Cather: A Memoir* (1953; Lincoln: University of Nebraska Press, 1963), 81–82.
6. Ibid., 85.
7. Willa Cather, *O Pioneers!* (1913; New York: Vintage Books, 1992), 158.
8. Willa Cather, *The Song of the Lark* (1915; Boston: Houghton Mifflin, 1983), 368.
9. Willa Cather, *Death Comes for the Archbishop* (1927; New York: Vintage Books, 1990), 21–22.
10. Rudnick, *Utopian Vistas*, 105.
11. Edith Lewis, *Willa Cather Living: A Personal Record* (New York: Alfred A. Knopf, 1953), 143.
12. Sergeant, *Willa Cather*, 235.
13. T. M. Pearce, *Literary America, 1903–1934: The Mary Austin Letters* (Westport, CT: Greenwood Press, 1979), 205.
14. Sergeant, *Willa Cather*, 226.
15. Pearce, *Literary America*, 171.

Chapter Six

1. Everett A. Gillis, *Oliver La Farge* (Austin, TX: Steck-Vaughn Co., 1967), 39.
2. From David L. Caffey, ed., introduction to *Yellow Sun, Bright Sky: The Indian Country Stories of Oliver La Farge* (Albuquerque: University of New Mexico Press, 1988), 5.
3. D'Arcy McNickle, *Indian Man: A Life of Oliver La Farge* (Bloomington: Indiana University Press, 1971), 5.
4. Ibid., 32–33.
5. From Caffey, *Yellow Sun, Bright Sky*, 2.
6. McNickle, *Indian Man*, 56.
7. Ibid., 58.
8. Ibid., 61.
9. Ibid., 64.
10. Caffey, *Yellow Sun, Bright Sky*, 4.
11. McNickle, *Indian Man*, 96.
12. Ibid., 104.
13. Ibid., 105.
14. Ibid., 69.
15. Ibid., 96.
16. Ibid., 124–25.
17. Ibid., 124.
18. Ibid., 133.
19. Ibid., 144–45.
20. Ibid., 237.

Chapter Seven

1. Luhan, *Edge of Taos Desert*, 6.
2. Rudnick, *Mabel Dodge Luhan*, 6.
3. Ibid., 16.
4. Ibid., 19.
5. Ibid., 17.
6. Ibid., 19.
7. Ibid., 23.
8. Ibid., 26.
9. Ibid., 33.
10. Ibid., 32.
11. Ibid., 33.
12. Ibid., 34.
13. Ibid., 33.
14. Ibid., 47.
15. Ibid., 47.
16. Ibid., 66.
17. Ibid., 49.
18. Ibid., 51.
19. Ibid., 39.
20. Ibid., 101.

21. Ibid., 102.
22. Ibid., 142.
23. Ibid., 145.
24. Luhan, *Edge of Taos Desert*, 23.
25. Ibid., 60.
26. Mabel Dodge Luhan, *Taos and Its Artists* (New York: Duell, Sloan and Pearce, 1947), 11.
27. Rudnick, *Mabel Dodge Luhan*, 149.
28. From Rudnick's introduction to Luhan, *Edge of Taos Desert*, xiv.
29. From my telephone interview with Rudnick on May 26, 2005.
30. Luhan, *Edge of Taos Desert*, 94.
31. Rudnick, *Mabel Dodge Luhan*, 176.
32. Rudnick, *Utopian Vistas*, 39.
33. Rudnick, *Mabel Dodge Luhan*, 183.
34. Ibid., 182.
35. Ibid.

Chapter Eight

1. Mabel Dodge Luhan, *Lorenzo in Taos* (New York: Alfred A. Knopf, 1932), 3.
2. Rudnick, *Mabel Dodge Luhan*, 193.
3. Ibid., 194.
4. Rudnick, *Utopian Vistas*, 100.
5. Ibid., 101.
6. Brenda Maddox, *D. H. Lawrence: The Story of a Marriage* (New York: Simon and Schuster, 1994), 315.
7. D. H. Lawrence, "Just Back from the Snake Dance—Tired Out," *Laughing Horse*, September 1924, n.p.
8. Rudnick, *Mabel Dodge Luhan*, 202.
9. Ibid., 209.
10. Luhan, *Lorenzo in Taos*, 69–70.
11. Rudnick, *Mabel Dodge Luhan*, 199.
12. Ibid.
13. Ibid., 201.
14. Ibid., 202.
15. Ibid., 195.
16. Luhan, *Lorenzo in Taos*, 278.
17. Ibid., 279.
18. Rudnick, *Mabel Dodge Luhan*, 249.
19. Maddox, *D. H. Lawrence*, 491.
20. Robert Lucas, *Frieda Lawrence: The Story of Frieda von Richthofen and D. H. Lawrence* (New York: Viking Press, 1973), 268.

Chapter Nine

1. Luhan, *Lorenzo in Taos*, 280.
2. Rudnick, *Utopian Vistas*, 152.
3. Rudnick, *Mabel Dodge Luhan*, 298.

4. Ibid., 256.
5. Ibid.
6. Ibid., 258.
7. Ibid., 259.
8. Ibid., 271.
9. Ibid., 267.
10. Earl Ganz, *The Taos Truth Game* (Albuquerque: University of New Mexico Press, 2006), 324.
11. Ibid., 325.
12. Ibid.
13. Rudnick, *Mabel Dodge Luhan*, 271.
14. Luhan, *Taos and Its Artists*, 11.

Chapter Ten

1. Sharyn L. Udall, *Spud Johnson & Laughing Horse* (Albuquerque: University of New Mexico Press, 1994), 97–98.
2. Ibid., 98.
3. Ibid., 102.
4. Ibid., 331.
5. Ibid., 118–99.
6. Ibid., 122.
7. Ibid., 129.
8. Ibid., 98.
9. Kraft, *Who Is Witter Bynner?*, 52.
10. Udall, *Spud Johnson & Laughing Horse*, 38.
11. Ibid., 155.
12. Kraft, *Who Is Witter Bynner?*, 53.
13. Udall, *Spud Johnson & Laughing Horse*, 15.
14. Ibid., 50.
15. Ibid., 53.
16. Ibid., 40.
17. Ibid., 63.
18. Claire Morrill, *A Taos Mosaic: Portrait of a New Mexico Village* (Albuquerque: University of New Mexico Press, 1973), 133.
19. Ibid.
20. Ibid.
21. Udall, *Spud Johnson & Laughing Horse*, 90.
22. Ibid.
23. From John Collier Jr.'s introduction to Luhan, *Edge of Taos Desert*, xxv.

Chapter Eleven

1. Frank Waters, *Of Time and Change: A Memoir* (Denver: MacMurray and Beck, 1998), 5.
2. From Rudolfo Anaya's introduction to Waters, *Of Time and Change*, xiii.
3. Ibid., 5.
4. Ibid., 11.
5. Ibid.

6. Rudnick, *Utopian Vistas*, 178.
7. Frank Waters, *Of Time and Change*, 26.
8. Ibid., 44.
9. Ibid., 13.
10. Ibid.
11. Frank Waters, *The Man Who Killed the Deer* (1942; Athens: Swallow Press/Ohio University Press, 1985), 261.
12. Barbara Waters, ed. *Rekindling the Inner Light: The Frank Waters Centennial* (Taos, NM: Frank Waters Foundation Press, 2003), 37.
13. Ibid., xix.
14. Ibid., 44.
15. Ibid., 190–91.
16. Ibid., 193.
17. Ibid., xix.
18. Frank Waters, *Of Time and Change*, 24.

Chapter Twelve

1. Braunlich, *Haunted by Home*, 6.
2. Ibid., 7.
3. Ibid., 8.
4. Ibid., 9
5. Ibid., 18.
6. Ibid., xi.
7. Ibid.
8. Ibid., 16.
9. Weigle and Fiore, *Santa Fe and Taos*, 51.
10. Ibid., 53.
11. Ibid., 136.
12. Kraft, *Who Is Witter Bynner?*, 93.
13. Ibid., 94.
14. Weigle and Fiore, *Santa Fe and Taos*, 62.
15. Ibid., 62–63.
16. Kraft, *Who Is Witter Bynner?*, 95.
17. Ibid., 95.
18. Haniel Long, "Cerrillos Hills," *Laughing Horse*, August 1925, n.p.
19. Robert Franklin Gish, *Beautiful Swift Fox: Erna Fergusson and the Modern Southwest* (College Station: Texas A&M University Press, 1996), 53.
20. Powell, *Southwest Classics*, 138.
21. Ibid., 143.
22. Gish, *Beautiful Swift Fox*, 78.
23. Powell, *Southwest Classics*, 60–61.
24. Ibid., 65.
25. Ibid., 67.
26. Ibid, 68.
27. From Robert Franklin Gish's afterword in Horgan, *The Centuries of Santa Fe*, 367.

28. Robert Franklin Gish, *Nueva Granada: Paul Horgan and the Southwest* (College Station: Texas A&M University Press, 1995), 73.
29. Genaro M. Padilla, ed., *The Short Stories of Fray Angelico Chavez* (1987; Albuquerque: University of New Mexico Press, 2003), viii.
30. Ibid.
31. Ibid., x.

Conclusion

1. Weigle and Fiore, *Santa Fe and Taos*, 39.
2. Rudnick, *Mabel Dodge Luhan*, 281.
3. Frank Waters, "Indian Influence on Taos Art," *New Mexico Quarterly Review*, Summer 1951, 178–79.
4. Brian Boyd, *Vladimir Nabokov: The American Years* (Princeton, NJ: Princeton University Press, 1991, 261.
5. Ibid.
6. Ibid.
7. Ibid.
8. Ibid., 262.
9. David King Dunaway and Sara Spurgeon, eds., *Writing the Southwest*, rev. ed. (Albuquerque: University of New Mexico Press, 2003), 1.
10. Ibid.
11. Dominick Dunne, "Greenwich Murder Time," *Vanity Fair*, June 2006, 82.
12. Norman Hales, *The Spider in the Cup* (New York: Signet, 1955), back cover.

Bibliography

Anaya, Rudolfo. *Serafina's Stories*. Albuquerque: University of New Mexico Press, 2004.

Austin, Mary. *Earth Horizon*. Boston: Houghton Mifflin, 1932.

———. "Frank Applegate." *New Mexico Quarterly Review*, August 1932, 213–18.

———. *The Land of Little Rain*. New York: Dover Publications, 1996 (1903).

Barrett, William P. "The Curse of Lew Wallace." Originally published in *Crosswinds Weekly*, May 1998. Expanded Internet version at members.aol.com/wmpb2/CrossWallace.

Boyd, Brian. *Vladimir Nabokov: The American Years*. Princeton, NJ: Princeton University Press, 1991.

Braunlich, Phyllis Cole. *Haunted by Home: The Life and Letters of Lynn Riggs*. Norman: University of Oklahoma Press, 1988.

Brett, Dorothy. *Lawrence and Brett: A Friendship*. Santa Fe: Sunstone Press, 2006 (1973).

Bynner, Witter. "Alice and I." *New Mexico Quarterly Review*, Spring 1949, 35–42.

———. *Cake: An Indulgence*. New York: Alfred A. Knopf, 1926.

———. *Journey with Genius: Recollections and Reflections Concerning the D. H. Lawrences*. New York: John Day, 1951.

———. *The Selected Witter Bynner: Poems, Plays, Translations, Prose and Letters*. Edited by James Kraft. Albuquerque: University of New Mexico Press, 1995.

Caffey, David L., ed. *Yellow Sun, Bright Sky: The Indian Country Stories of Oliver La Farge*. Albuquerque: University of New Mexico Press, 1988.

Cather, Willa. *Death Comes for the Archbishop*. New York: Vintage Books, 1990 (1927).

————. *My Antonia*. Boston: Houghton Mifflin, 1977 (1918).

————. *O, Pioneers!* New York: Vintage Books, 1992 (1913).

————. *The Song of the Lark*. Boston: Houghton Mifflin, 1983 (1915).

Church, Peggy Pond. *The House at Otowi Bridge: The Story of Edith Warner and Los Alamos*. Albuquerque: University of New Mexico Press, 1959, 1960.

Coke, Van Deren. *Taos and Santa Fe: The Artist's Environment 1882–1942*. Albuquerque: University of New Mexico Press for The Amon Carter Museum of Western Art and The Art Gallery, University of New Mexico, 1963.

Day, James. M. *Paul Horgan*. Austin: Steck-Vaughn Co., 1967.

DeWitt, Miriam Hapgood. *Taos: A Memory*. Albuquerque: University of New Mexico Press, 1992.

Dunaway, David King, and Sara Spurgeon, eds. *Writing the Southwest*. Rev. ed. Albuquerque: University of New Mexico Press, 2003.

Dunne, Dominick. "Greenwich Murder Time." *Vanity Fair*, June 2006, 82–83.

Ganz, Earl. *The Taos Truth Game*. Albuquerque: University of New Mexico Press, 2006.

Gillis, Everett A. *Oliver La Farge*. Austin, TX: Steck-Vaughn Co., 1967.

Gish, Robert Franklin. *Beautiful Swift Fox: Erna Fergusson and the Modern Southwest*. College Station: Texas A&M University Press, 1996.

————. *Nueva Granada: Paul Horgan and the Southwest*. College Station: Texas A&M University Press, 1995.

Grant, Blanche C. *When Old Trails Were New: The Story of Taos*. Glorieta, NM: The Rio Grande Press, 1983 (1934).

Hales, Norman. *The Spider in the Cup*. New York: Signet, 1955.

The Harwood Foundation of the University of New Mexico. *Taos: 1923–1933: A Brief History and Collection Listing Published on the Seventieth Anniversary of the Foundation*. Taos: Harwood Foundation, 1993.

Henderson, Alice Corbin. "Literature." *New Mexico: A Guide to the Colorful State*. New York: Hastings House, 1940, 130–40.

————. *Red Earth, Poems of New Mexico*. Compiled and edited by Lois Rudnick and Ellen Zieselman. Santa Fe: Museum of New Mexico Press, 2003; originally published as *Red Earth: Poems of New Mexico*. Chicago: Ralph Fletcher Seymour, 1920.

————, ed. *The Turquoise Trail: An Anthology of New Mexico Poetry*. Boston: Houghton Mifflin, 1928.

Horgan, Paul. *The Centuries of Santa Fe*. Albuquerque: University of New Mexico Press, 1994.

Johnson, Spud. *Horizontal Yellow*. Santa Fe: Rydal Press, 1935.

Kraft, James. *Who Is Witter Bynner?* Albuquerque: University of New Mexico Press, 1995.

La Farge, John Pen. *Turn Left at the Sleeping Dog: Scripting the Santa Fe Legend 1920–1955*. Albuquerque: University of New Mexico Press, 2001.

La Farge, Oliver. *Laughing Boy*. New York: Signet Classics, 1971 (1929).

————. *The Man with the Calabash Pipe*. Boston: Houghton Mifflin, 1966.

————. *Yellow Sun, Bright Sky: The Indian Country Stories of Oliver La*

Farge. Edited by David L. Caffey. Albuquerque: University of New Mexico Press. 1988.

Lawrence, D. H. *The Complete Short Stories*. Vol. 1. New York: Viking Press, 1976 (1961).

———. "Just Back from the Snake Dance—Tired Out." *Laughing Horse*, September 1924, n.p.

———. *Mornings in Mexico and Etruscan Places*. London: Heinemann, 1956.

———. *The Plumed Serpent (Quetzalcoatl)*. New York: Alfred A. Knopf, 1926.

Lawrence, Frieda. *"Not I, But the Wind . . ."* Carbondale: Southern Illinois University Press, 1974 (1934).

Lewis, Edith. *Willa Cather Living: A Personal Record*. New York: Alfred A. Knopf, 1953.

Long, Haniel. "Cerrillos Hills." *Laughing Horse*, August 1925, n.p.

Lucas, Robert. *Frieda Lawrence: The Story of Frieda von Richthofen and D. H. Lawrence*. New York: Viking Press, 1973.

Luhan, Mabel Dodge. *Edge of Taos Desert*. Albuquerque: University of New Mexico Press, 1987 (1937).

———. *Lorenzo in Taos*. New York: Alfred A. Knopf, 1932.

———. *Taos and Its Artists*. New York: Duell, Sloan and Pearce, 1947.

Luther, T. N. *Collecting Santa Fe Authors*. Santa Fe: Ancient City Press, 2002.

———. *Collecting Taos Authors*. Albuquerque: New Mexico Book League, 1993.

Lyday, Jo W. *Mary Austin*. Austin, TX: Steck-Vaughn Co., 1968.

Maddox, Brenda. *D. H. Lawrence: The Story of a Marriage*. New York: Simon and Schuster, 1994.

Marling, Karal Ann. Introduction to *Woodstock: An American Art Colony, 1902–1977*. Poughkeepsie, NY: Vassar College Art Gallery, 1977.

McNickle, D'Arcy. *Indian Man: A Life of Oliver La Farge*. Bloomington: Indiana University Press, 1971.

Morrill, Claire. *A Taos Mosaic: Portrait of a New Mexico Village*. Albuquerque: University of New Mexico Press, 1973.

O'Brien, Sharon. *Willa Cather: The Emerging Voice*. New York: Ballantine, 1989.

Otis, Raymond. *Fire in the Night*. New York: Farrar and Rinehart, 1934.

Padget, Martin. *Indian Country: Travels in the American Southwest 1840–1935*. Albuquerque: University of New Mexico Press, 2004.

Padilla, Genaro M., ed. *The Short Stories of Fray Angelico Chavez*. Albuquerque: University of New Mexico Press, 2003 (1987).

Pearce, T. M. *Alice Corbin Henderson*. Austin, TX: Steck-Vaughn Co., 1969.

———, ed. *Literary America, 1903–1934: The Mary Austin Letters*. Westport, CT: Greenwood Press, 1979.

Powell, Lawrence Clark. *Southwest Classics*. Pasadena, CA: Ward Ritchie Press, 1975 (1974).

Riskin, Marci L. *The Train Stops Here: New Mexico's Railway Legacy*. Albuquerque: University of New Mexico Press, 2005.

Rudnick, Lois Palken. *Mabel Dodge Luhan: New Woman, New World*s. Albuquerque: University of New Mexico Press, 2000 (1984).

———. *Utopian Vistas: The Mabel Dodge Luhan House and the American Counterculture*. Albuquerque: University of New Mexico Press, 1996.

Sergeant, Elizabeth Shepley. "The Santa Fe Group." *Saturday Review of Literature*, December 8, 1934.

———. *Willa Cather: A Memoir*. Lincoln: University of Nebraska Press, 1963 (1953).

Sherman, John. *Santa Fe: A Pictorial History*. Norfolk, VA.: Donning Co., 1983.

Silverman, Jason. *Untold New Mexico: Stories from a Hidden Past*. Santa Fe: Sunstone Press, 2006.

Smith, Pamela S. Smith, with Richard Polese. *Passions in Print: Private Press Artistry in New Mexico, 1834–Present*. Santa Fe: Museum of New Mexico Press, 2006.

Stevenson, Philip. "Santa Fe: A Study in Integrity." *New Mexico Quarterly Review*, August 1933, 125–32.

Stineman, Esther Lanigan. *Mary Austin: Song of a Maverick*. New Haven: Yale University Press, 1989.

Udall, Sharyn R. *Spud Johnson & Laughing Horse*. Albuquerque: University of New Mexico Press, 1994.

Waters, Barbara, ed. *Rekindling the Inner Light: The Frank Waters Centennial*. Taos, NM: The Frank Waters Foundation Press, 2003.

Waters, Frank. "Indian Influence on Taos Art." *New Mexico Quarterly Review*, Summer 1951, 173–80.

———. *The Man Who Killed the Deer*. Athens: Swallow Press/Ohio University Press, 1985 (1942).

———. *Of Time and Change: A Memoir*. Denver: MacMurray and Beck, 1998.

———. *The Woman at Otowi Crossing*. Athens: Swallow Press/Ohio University Press, 1987 (1966).

Weigle, Marta, and Kyle Fiore. *Santa Fe and Taos: The Writer's Era, 1916–1941*. Santa Fe: Ancient City Press, 1982.

Wilson, Chris. *The Myth of Santa Fe: Creating a Modern Regional Tradition*. Albuquerque: University of New Mexico Press, 1997.

Index

Page numbers in bold type indicate photos or illustrations.

Abbey, Edward, 149
Accidental Magic (Church), 123
Acoma Pueblo, 108
Adams, Ansel, x, 98, 100, 155, 162
Alexander's Bridge (Cather), 56
Alexie, Sherman, 9
Altitude (Lawrence), 110
American Association of Indian Affairs, 68
American Mercury, 129, 138
American Rhythm, 45
Anaya, Rudolfo, 10, 119
Anderson, Sherwood, 110
Andrews' Harvest (Henderson), 75
Anglos, 25, 137, 138
Anthology of Magazine Verse and Yearbook of American Poetry, 111
Apache Indians, 65
Applegate, Frank, 49, 145, 154
April Twilights (Cather), 55, 56
Armitage, Shelly, 123
Arnold, Matthew, 75
Arrow Editions, 26
The Arrow-Maker (Austin), 46
Arsuna School of Fine Arts, 49
assimilation policy, 66, 67
Atlantic Monthly, 44

Atlantides (Long), 27, 134
Austin, Mary, x, 42–47, **47**, 58, 59, 107, 112, 122, 123, 132; article opposing Bursum Bill, 86; and escape from urban life, 3; forms literary colony in California, 46; founds Santa Fe Community Theater, 155; house of, 152–54; influence of New Mexico landscape on, 25; Lummis as mentor to, 15; portrait of, **43**; as reader at Poets' Roundup, 26; serves as judge on panel for Pulitzer Prize, 64; suffers nervous breakdown, 45; as worshiper of Native American culture, 110
Austin, Wallace, 44
Authentic Life of Billy the Kid (Garrett), 14

Baca, Consuelo, 68
Baca, Jimmy Santiago, 151
Background (Luhan), 97
ballads, 10, 112
Bandelier, Adolph, 8, 136
Bandelier National Monument, 136
The Basket Woman (Austin), 46
Baumann, Gustave, 48, 155
Behind the Mountain, 69
Ben Hur (Wallace), 14, 15
Bierce, Ambrose, 46

Billy the Kid, 14
Bishop's Lodge (Lamy's retreat), 152, 157
Bishop's Lodge Resort & Spa, 157
Blanche, Jacques-Émile, 76
The Blood of the Conquerors (Harvey), 138
Blumenschein, Ernest L., iii, **143**
Bohr, Neils, 123
Bones Incandescent: The Pajarito Journals of Peggy Pond Church, 123
Bonney, William, 14
Book of Lyrics (Bynner), 40
The Book of the Hopi (Deloria), 121
book publishing, 26
Boulder Dam Conference, 49
Bradlee, Ben, 150
Braunlich, Phyllis Cole, 128
The Brave Cowboy (Abbey), 149
Brett, Dorothy, **94**, 95, 164
Brill, A. A., 78, 101
Brinig, Myron, 99–101, 120
Brothers of the Light: The Penitentes of the Southwest (Henderson), 27
Bureau of Indian Affairs, 66
Burlin, Paul, 80, 154
Burns, Patrick, 123
Burroughs, William S., 122
Bursum, Holm Olaf, 85
Bursum Bill, 28, 48, 65, 85–86, 107; writers band together to defeat, 25
Bynner, Witter, x, 23, 28, 29–41, 42, 80, 91–92, 99, 104–5, 107, 112, 128, 129, 133, 137, **139**; Asian influence on, 32–33; drawing of Lawrence, **36**; and escape from urban life, 3; and fiesta parade, 156; and homosexuality, 36, 39; house of, 154–55; influence of New Mexico landscape on, 25; joins Fiske to create Spectra Hoax, 31; with the Lawrences, **30**; and negative publicity, 33; as reader at Poets' Roundup, 26; relationship with Johnson, 110; relationship with Lawrence, 38, 155; relationship with Long, 134; Robert Frost angers, 16; suffers stroke, 40

Caffey, David L., 63
Cake: An Indulgence (Bynner), 37, 38, 99
Camino del Monte Sol, 23, 42, 49
Canfield, Dorothy, 54
Capote, Truman, 150
Carson, Kit, 160, 162
"Casa Luhan, Taos" (watercolor), 84
Casa Querida, 154
Cassidy, Gerald, 48, 130
Cassidy, Ina Sizer, 48, 130
Cather, Willa, ix, 13, 52–60, **53**, 138, 140, 154, 156, 157, 162; and Albuquerque, 56; anger over changes to her story made by Bynner, 30; and escape from urban life, 3
Catholic Church, 13, 59; and Penitentes, 27
The Centuries of Santa Fe (Horgan), 142
"Cerrillos Hills" (Hunt), 135
Chanslor, Roy, 105, 107
Chappell, Warren, 26
Chávez, Angélico, 142–44, **143**
Chávez, Manuel Ezequiel, 144
Chiaroscuro Gallery, 152
Chicano literature, 144
Church, Kathleen, 123
Church, Peggy Pond, 26, 27, 122, 123, 134, 137, 162
Clark, L. D., 90–91
Clothed with the Sun (Chávez), 144
Cochise (La Farge), 69
Cochiti Pueblo, 41
Cody, William "Buffalo Bill," 158
Collier, John, 67, 77, 85, 107, 116
Colorado Post, 86
Colter, Mary, 156, 158
Commerce on the Prairies (Gregg), 12
Connell, Evan S., 151
The Conquest of Don Pedro (Fergusson), 140
Conservationist magazine, 145
Cuaderno de Ortografi, 13
cuentos, 10
Curtis, Natalie, 80
Cutting, Bronson, 110

"A Dance of Rain" (Bynner), 41
Dancing Gods (Fergusson), 137
Dasburg, Andrew, 77
Davis, Bette, 99
Davis, Jon, 151
Davis, W.W. H., 12
Death Comes for the Archbishop (Cather), 13, 52, 58, 59, 138, 154, 157
The Delight-Makers (Bandelier), 8
Del Monte Ranch, 91
Deloria, Vine, 121
Desert Solitaire (Abbey), 149
The Dial, 64
Dodge, Edwin, 75, 77
Douglas, Kirk, 149
Duncan, Isadora, 77

Earth Horizon (Austin), 48, 50
Eastern Association of Indian Affairs, 65
Eastman, Ida Rauh, 130
Eastman, Max, 77, 130
Eden Tree (Bynner), 39
Edge of Taos Desert (Luhan), 74, 79–80, 82, 97, 98, 101, 116, 161
El Gringo; Or, New Mexico and Her People (Davis), 12
Eliot, T. S., 144
El Ortiz (Harvey House), 158
Emory, William, 12
The Enemy Gods (La Farge), 66
Erdrich, Louise, 9
Espanola, NM, 57
European Experiences (Luhan), 76, 97
Evans, John, 28
Evans, Kirk, 75
Experiences Facing Death (Austin), 44

Fantazius Mallare (Hecht), 106
Faulkner, William, 64
Ferber, Edna, 16
Fergusson, Erna, 134, 135, **136**, 137
Fergusson, Harvey, 135, **139**
Fergusson, Harvey Butler (congressman), 135
Fever Pitch (Waters), 119
Ficke, Arthur Davison, 31
Fiore, Kyle, x
Fire in the Night (Otis), 36, 132
Fletcher, John Gould, 27

The Flock (Austin), 46
Flynn, Errol, 99, 155
folklore, 146
Foretaste (Church), 27
Frank Waters Foundation, 124
Fremstad, Olive, 57
Frijoles Canyon Pictographs (Baumann), 27
Frost, Robert, 16, 35, 155

Ganson, Charles, 74
Ganson, Sara Cook, 74
Ganz, Earl, 99, 100
Garrett, Pat F., 14
General Federation of Women's Clubs, 85
Gish, Robert Franklin, 137, 140
Glazner, Gary Mex, 151
Glazner, Greg, 151
Goldman, Emma, 77
Goodwin, Walter Lippincott, Jr., 26, 27
The Goose Step: A Study of American Education, 107
Graham, Martha, 155, 162
Grant, Cary, 138
Great River: The Rio Grande in North American History (Horgan), 142
Green Grow the Lilacs (Riggs), 129
Gregg, Josiah, 12
Griffith, D. W., 100

Hacienda del Sol, 160
Hales, Norman, 150
Hansel and Gretel, 100
Harjo, Linda, 9
Harvey, Fred, 137, 156
Harvey Houses, 16, 156, 158
Harvey Indian Detours, 137
Harwood, Burt: house of, 162
Harwood Foundation, 102, 162
Harwood Museum of Art, 162
"Haunted Ground" (La Farge), 66
Hayes, Rutherford B., 14
Hayworth, Rita, 155
Hecht, Ben, 106
Henderson, Alice Corbin, x, 5, 12, 14, 18, **20**, 21–28, 29, 42, 75, 80, 137, 152; and Albert Pike, 11; article opposing Bursum Bill, 86; and beginning of Santa Fe literary colony, 4; first meeting

with Bynner, 33; promotion of New Mexico, 25; and tuberculosis, 2, 21–22
Henderson, Alice (daughter), 28, 33
Henderson, William Penhallow, **20**, 22, 23, 33, 75
Henry, O., 29, 35, 154
Hickey, Ethel, 136
Hispanos, 25, 34, 138, 144
"Historia de la Nueva Mexico," 9
Hogan, Linda, 9
Home in the West: An Inquiry into My Origins (Fergusson), 140
Home Monthly magazine, 55
homosexuality, 36, 39, 113
Hoover, Herbert, 46
Hopi Indians, 67, 121
Horgan, Paul, 3, 39, 134, 137, 140–42, **141**
Horizontal Yellow, 112
The Horse Fly, 103, 113–14, 160
Hot Saturday (Harvey), 138
The House at Otowi Bridge (Church), 122–23
House Made of Dawn (Momaday), 9
Howlett, W. J., 58
Huning, Franz, 140
Hunt, Myron, 154
Hunt, Robert, 39, 40, 135, 154

Imagist school, 24, 33
Indian Arts Fund, 49
Indian Earth (Bynner), 40–41
Indian poetry, 112
Indian Reorganization Act of 1934, 67
Indian rights, 50
Indian Stories from the Pueblos (Applegate), 49
influenza, 29
Inn of the Turquoise Bear, 155
Interlinear to Cabeza de Vaca (Long), 134
"In the Quiet Night" (Li Po), 32
In the Shadow of Los Alamos: Selected Writings of Edith Warner, 123
In Those Days: An Impression of Change (Fergusson), 140
Intimate Memories (Luhan), 74, 97
Isidro (Austin), 46

Jade Mountain (Bynner), 32
James, William, 45
Jeffers, Robinson, 96, 162
Jewett, Sarah Orne, 56, 60
Jicarilla Reservation, 65
Johnson, Willard "Spud," 18, 19, 23, 37, 38, 39, 92, 100, 103–16, **104**, **115**, 162; and art, 114; house of, 158–59; poetry of, 111–12; relationship with Bynner, 110
Journey with Genius: Recollections and Reflections Concerning the D. H. Lawrences (Bynner), 38, 155
"Just back from the Snake-Dance— Tired Out" (Lawrence), 89

Karavas, James and John, 163
Karavas, Saki, 163
Kelsey printing press, 110, 116
Kiang Kang-hu, 32–33
Kimball, Clark, 27
Kiowa Ranch, 92, 93, 94, 95, 163, 164
Kit Carson Historic Cemetery, 102, 160
Koshare Indians, 8
Koshare Tours, 136, 137
Kraft, James, 30, 31, 32, 35, 37, 38, 39, 40, 41, 110, 111, 133

Lady Chatterley's Lover (Lawrence), 93, 110, 163
La Farge, Oliver, 18, 28, 61–69, **62**, 152; columns about Santa Fe life, 17; and Consuelo Baca, 68
La Fonda de Taos, 163
La Fonda Hotel, **2**, 2, 16, 58, 59, 156, 157
Lamy, Jean Baptiste, 13, 52, 58, 156, 158; grave of, 157; statue of, 157. *See also* Bishop's Lodge
Lamy, NM, 2, 94, 127, 152, 157–58
Lamy of Santa Fe: His Life and Times (Horgan), 142
The Land of Journey's Ending (Austin), 16, 48
The Land of Little Rain (Austin), 16, 44, 45–46, 48, 50
The Land of Poco Tiempo (Lummis), 15, 16, 45
The Land of the Pueblos (Wallace), 15

Lannan Foundation, 150
Laughing Boy (La Farge), 17, 61, 64
The Laughing Horse Inn, 112, 160
Laughing Horse magazine, 12,
    37, 89, 103, 105, 107, 108–9,
    112, 116, 129, 158, 160;
    advertisements in, **2**, **146**;
    Bynner's drawing of Lawrence in,
    36; and censorship, 110; covers
    of, **106**, **107**; drawings from, 6
Lawrence, D. H., ix, 5, 37, 85–86,
    87–95, **88**, 97, 100, 105–6,
    109, 110, 111, 152, 155; with
    Bynner, **30**; disposition of ashes,
    94–95; drawing by, **6**; and escape
    from urban life, 3; Hacienda
    del Sol and, 160; influence of
    New Mexico landscape on, 25;
    oil paintings by, 163; paints
    windows at Los Gallos, 162; pen
    and ink drawing by Bynner, **36**;
    ranch of, 164; relationship with
    Bynner, 38, 155; relationship
    with Luhan, 90
Lawrence, Frieda, **30**, 37, 38, 39, 89,
    90, 92, 93, **94**, 95, 100, 109, 110,
    134, 155, 163; relationship with
    Luhan, 94–95
*The Laws of the Territory of
    New Mexico*, 13
Levin, Dana, 151
Lewis, Edith, 56, 57
*The Life of the Right Reverend
    Joseph P. Machebeuf—Pioneer
    Priest of New Mexico* (Howlett),
    58
Lincoln County Wars, 14
Lindsay, Vachel, 16, 31
Li Po, 32
Lippmann, Walter, 77
literary colonies: beginnings of, 18;
    fading and disappearance of, 145;
    layered history of, x
literary gatherings, 16
literature: federal aid for, 146–47;
    magical realism in, 149
Little Valley (Otis), 132
Lobo Ranch, 92, 164
Logghe, Joan, 151
London, Jack, 46
Lonely Are the Brave (film), 149

Long, Haniel, 23, 27, 107, 132–35,
    133, 137; as reader at Poets'
    Roundup, 26; relationship with
    Bynner, 134
Long Pennant (La Farge), 66
Lorenzo in Taos (Luhan), 87, 92, 93,
    96
Los Alamos, NM, 147
Los Alamos Ranch School, 122
Los Gallos, 73, 83, 100, 102, 110,
    119, 161–62
A Lost Lady (Cather), 55
Lovett, Sarah, 151
Lowell, Amy, 31
Lucas, Robert, 93
Luhan, Mabel Dodge, x, 18, 28, 42,
    46, 47, 48, 50, 58, **72**, 73–86, 93,
    94, 96–102, **97**, 105, 113, 116,
    137, 163; and beginning of Taos
    literary colony, 4; Brinig buys
    property from, 100; burial site of,
    160; childhood of, 74; contracts
    syphilis, 83; and funding of
    hospital, 122; Hacienda del Sol
    and, 160; on horseback, **78**;
    house of, 161–62; influence of
    New Mexico landscape on, 25;
    Johnson visits, 109; Lawrence
    on ego of, 89; as leader of
    opposition to Bursum Bill, 107;
    on Martínez, 13; and Native
    American culture, 79; and
    Native American rights, 85; not
    invited to go on Mexico trip, 37,
    110; portrayal in Bynner play,
    99; relationship with Bynner,
    38; relationship with D. H.
    Lawrence, 90; relationship with
    Frieda Lawrence, 94–95; rents
    house from Manby, 161; trades
    ranch for Lawrence manuscript,
    92, 164; as worshiper of Native
    American culture, 110
Luhan, Tony, 58, **81**, 82, 86, **97**,
    102, 119; and peyote, 101; and
    syphilis, 83
Luhan, Una, 96–97
Lummis, Charles, 15, 45
Lumpkin, William, **17**, **70**

Machebeuf, Joseph P., 58
Macleod, Norman, 130–31
Maddox, Brenda, 93

Manby, Arthur Rochford, 81; burial site of, 161; house of, 161
The Man Who Killed the Deer (Waters), 120–21, 160
The Man with the Calabash Pipe (La Farge), 69
Marcy, Randolph B., 12
Marling, Karal Ann, 4
Martínez, Antonio José, 12–14, 144, 160
Martinez, Valerie, 151
The Masses magazine, 78
Matthews, Wanden, 65
McCarthy, Cormac, 151
McClung, Isabel, 55, 56, 57
McClure's Magazine, 29–30, 55, 56, 57
McClure, S. S., 55
McNickle, D'Arcy, 63, 68
Meem, John Gaw, 156, 162
Mencken, H. L., 138
Mera, Frank, 21, 23
Merrild, Knud, 91
Meyers, Ralph, 160
Miguel of the Bright Mountain (Otis), 132
The Milagro Beanfield War (Nichols), 149
Millay, Edna St. Vincent, 31
Miller, Henry, 135
Momaday, N. Scott, 9
Monroe, Harriett, 21
Morley, Sylvanus, **143**
"Morning Walk—Santa Fe" (Riggs), 129
Morrell, David, 151
Morrill, Claire, 114
The Mother Ditch (La Farge), 69
"The Mother of Felipe," 45
Movers and Shakers (Luhan), 97
"mud-hut nuts," 36
murals, **17**, **70**, 144
Murder and Mystery in New Mexico (Fergusson), 137
Museum of Navaho Ceremonial Art, 28
My Antonia (Cather), 55
mythology, 46

Nabokov, Vladimir, 148–49
National Popular Government League, 86
The Nation magazine, 25

Native American rights, 85, 111
Native Americans, 34; La Farge's focus on, 61; and stories, 9
Native Tales from New Mexico (Austin), 49
Navajo Indians, 63, 66, 119, 129
Navarro, Ramon, 65
Nebraska State Journal, 54
New Mexico: appeal of, to writers and artists, 3; Henderson's promotion of, 25; history of, 34; as locale from which to recover from tuberculosis, 3; no longer a sanctuary, 147; three cultures of, 142; and tourism, 1, 27; and trade, 10
New Mexico: A Guide to the Colorful State (Henderson), 11, 27, 146
New Mexico (American Recreational Series), 146–47
New Mexico, a Pageant of Three Peoples (Fergusson), 137
"New Mexico" (Lawrence), 89
New Mexico: The Sunshine State's Recreational and Highway Magazine, 145
New Mexico Association on Indian Affairs, 25, 26
New Mexico Cafe, 16
"The New Mexico Cafe" (Bynner), 16
New Mexico Federal Writers' Project, 130, 146
New Mexico Highway Journal, 145
New Mexico Magazine, 145
New Mexico Military Institute, 142
New Mexico Museum, 16
New Mexico Quarterly Review, 28, 49, 145
New Mexico Sentinel, 134
"The New Mexico Writers' Page," 134
New Mexico Writers' Program, 146
New Poems 1960 (Bynner), 40
New Republic magazine, 25, 111, 129
The New World (Bynner), 30
New Yorker, 17, 67, 69, 112, 113
New York Times, 86
Nichols, John, 149
Nizalowski, John, 121, 124
"North Is Black" (La Farge), 64
Not I, But the Wind (Lawrence), 93

An Ode to Harvard and Other Poems (Bynner), 30
Of Time and Change (Waters), 119
O. Henry Award, 66
O'Keeffe, Georgia, x, 77, 98, 113, 162
Oklahoma! (Rogers and Hammerstein), 129
Oñate, Juan de, 9
One of Ours (Cather), 52
O'Neill, Eugene, 130
O Pioneers! (Cather), 57
Oppenheimer, Robert, 123
O'Shea, John, 150
Otis, Raymond, 26, 27, 36, 130, **131**
Our Town (Wilder), 98
Overland Monthly, 45

Padilla, Genaro, 144
Palace of the Governors, 10, 14
Park, George, 16
parody, 50
Pearce, T. M., 59
Penitentes, 27, 144
People of the Valley (Waters), 160
"The Perambulator" (Johnson), 113
Perkins, Maxwell, 110
Phoenix: The Posthumous Papers (Lawrence), 89
Pike, Albert, 11
Pike's Peak, 117
Pittsburgh Leader, 55
Pittsburgh Memoranda, 134
Pittsburgh Post, 86
plays, 155; religious, 10
The Plumed Serpent (Lawrence), 39, 92
A Poet and Two Painters (Merrild), 91
Poetry magazine, 21, 80, 111, 122
"Poets and Indians in Politics" (Johnson), 107
Poets' Roundup, 26, 49, 134
Pond, Ashley, 122
Porter, Eliot, 114
"The Portrait of Mabel Dodge Luhan at the Villa Curonia" (Stein), 76
Pound, Ezra, 24
Powell, Lawrence Clark, 48, 137, 140
Prose Sketches and Poems, Written in the Western Country (Pike), 11
Protest of Artists and Writers Against the Bursum Bill, 85

Proust, Marcel, 98
Pueblo ceremonial dances, 35
"Pueblo Indian Dancers," **6**
Pueblo Indians, 8, 25, 34, 85, 109; Spanish reconquest of, 156
Pueblo Revolt of 1680, 10, 34

Quetzalcoatl (Lawrence), 92

The Rabble, 23
Rabelais, François, 23
Ramage, Adam, 12
Ramage press, 12, 13, 14
Rananim, 87, 91
Ravagli, Angelo, 93, 94, 163, 164
Red Earth: Poems of New Mexico (Henderson), 24
Reed, John, 77
Remembrance of Things Past (Proust), 98
Rensselaer, James Van, Jr., 105
Riggs, Lynn, 16, 23, 107, 127–30
Rio Grande (Fergusson), 140
Robey, Roberta, 113
Rogers, Millicent, 38
Rönneback, Arnold, 84
Roosevelt, Franklin, 67, 146
Rudnick, Lois Palken, x, 3, 27–28, 38, 46, 50, 58, 74, 76, 77, 82, 83, 86, 89, 90, 98, 101, 119; on Santa Fe lifestyle, 23
Rydal Press, 26, 27, 146

Sagan, Miriam, 151
Saint Francis Cathedral, 156–57
Samora, Frank, 120
"Sanatarium" (Riggs), 129
sanatoriums, 21
Sandburg, Carl, 22, 31, 110
Sandoval, Joe Ray, 151
Sanger, Margaret, 77, 130
Sangre de Cristo Mountains, 1, 34
San Ildefonso Pueblo, 122
Santa Clara Pueblo, 65
Santa Fe, NM: beginning of art colony in, 4; elevation of, 3; and hippies, 149; as second largest art market, 150; Spanish Colonial background, 9–10; Spanish reconquest of, 34; and tourism, 1, 5; walking/driving tour map of, **153**
Santa Fe Fiesta, 34, 156

"The Santa Fe Gadfly," 114
"The Santa Fe Group" (Sergeant), 132
Santa Fe Indian Market, 25
Santa Fe Little Theater, 48, 155
Santa Fe New Mexican, 17, 67, 69, 113, 114
Santa Fe Playhouse, 48, 155
Santa Fe Plaza, 155–56
Santa Fe Plaza: A Weekly News Magazine of Old Santa Fe, 18
Santa Fe Southern Railway, 158
Santa Fe Trail, 2, 10, 12, 155
Santa Fe Trail (film), 155
Santo Domingo Pueblo, 80
Santuario de Chimayó, 49
Sarton, May, 123, 135
satire, 50
Saturday Review of Literature, 35, 122, 132
School of American Research, 23
Scott, Winfield Townley, 69
"The Secret of War" (Luhan), 78
"Self-Dependence" (Arnold), 75
Sergeant, Elizabeth Shipley, 35, 56, 57, 59, 71, 132; article opposing Bursum Bill, 86
Shadows Flying (Henderson), 75
The Short Stories of Fray Angélico Chávez, 144
Silko, Leslie Marmon, 9
Simpson, Smith, 162
Sinclair, Upton, 107, 110
The Sisters (film), 99
Sitgreaves, Lorenzo, 12
Six Taoseños Who Braved the Colorado Rivers (Johnson and Merrill), 114
Sloan, Dolly, 34, 156
Sloan, John, x, 34
The Song of the Lark (Cather), 57
songs, 10, 111, 155; folk, 24; religious, 27
Sons and Lovers (Lawrence), 87, 92, 164
Southwest Classics (Powell), 48
Southwestern Association on Indian Affairs, 25
Southwest Research Center, 163
The Spanish-American Song and Game Book, 147
Spanish Colonial Arts Society, 49
Sparks Fly Upward (La Farge), 66

Spectra hoax, 31, 107
The Spider in the Cup (Hales), 150
Spud Johnson & Laughing Horse (Udall), 37, 104
Starry Adventure (Austin), 50
Steffens, Lincoln, 77
Steiglitz, Alfred, 77
Stein, Gertrude, 76–77
Stein, Leo, 76, 77
The Sterile Cuckoo (Nichols), 149
Sterling, George, 46
Sterne, Maurice, 78, 79
Stineman, Esther Lanigan, 42, 45–46
Stokowski, Leopold, 98
storytelling, 28
Sunmount Sanitorium, 21, 22, 33, 128, 129
The Sun Turns West (Henderson), 26
syphilis, 83
Sze, Arthur, 151

T'ang poems, 32–33
Taos, NM: and hippies, 149; Luhan publicizes, 97; and tourism, 1, 5, 101, 148; walking/driving tour map of, **159**
Taos and Its Artists (Luhan), 80, 101
Taos Book Shop, 114
Taos Open Forum, 98
Taos Pueblo, 9–10, 79, 101, 112; music of, 98
The Taos Truth Game (Ganz), 99, 100
Taos Valley News, 113
Tarn, Nathaniel, 151
Tesuque village, 26
Tilano, 123
Toklas, Alice B., 76
To Possess the Land (Waters), 161
The Troll Garden (Cather), 55
tuberculosis, 2, 3, 21, 22, 33, 50, 92, 129
Tucker, Lisa, 151
Turner, Frederick, 151
The Turquoise Trail, An Anthology of New Mexico Poetry (Henderson), 25

Udall, Sharyn, 37, 104, 113
University of New Mexico, 28, 146, 162, 163, 164
Ute Indians, 119

Vechten, Carl Van, 77
Velez, Lupe, 65
Vidal, Gore, 122
Vierra, Carlos, 48, 155
Villa Curonia, 76
Villagrá, Gaspar Peréz de, 9
Villagra Bookshop, 113
Villa Pintoresca, 157
The Virgin of Port Lligat (Chávez), 144

Wallace, Lew, 14
Wallace, Susan E., 15
Warner, Edith, 121–22, 123
Waters, Barbara, 124
Waters, Frank, 116–24, **118**, 147, 160, 161
The Way of Life according to Laotzu: An American Version (Bynner), 32
Weigle, Marta, x
Welch, Jim, 9
Wells, Cady, 100
Wheelwright, Mary Cabot, 28
Wheelwright Museum of the American Indians, 23, 28
Where the Cross Is Made (O'Neill), 130
Wide Open Town (Brinig), 100
Wilder, Thornton, 16, 98, 99, 162

Willa Cather: A Memoir (Sergeant), 56, 57
Willa Cather Living (Lewis), 58
Williams, William Carlos, 40
Winter in Taos (Luhan), 101
Witter Bynner Foundation for Poetry, 40
Wolfe, Thomas, 98, 99
Wolf Song (Harvey), 138
Woman at Otowi Crossing (Waters), 123
Woman of Genius (Austin), 46
"The Woman Who Rode Away" (Lawrence), 91
women's rights, 49, 50
Woodstock Art Colony, 4
Works Progress Administration, 27, 146
A World of Light: Portraits and Celebrations (Sarton), 135
Writers' Editions, 26, 27, 112, 122, 132, 134

XXIV Elegies (Fletcher), 27

Yellow Sun, Bright Sun (La Farge), 63
You and I (Brinig), 100
Young, Vernon, 150

Zia Pueblo, 50